teach yourself®

helping your child to read

helping your child to read

dee reid and diana bentley

Launched in 1938, the **teach yourself** series
grew rapidly in response to the world's wartime
needs. Loved and trusted by over 50 million
readers, the series has continued to respond to
society's changing interests and passions and
now, 70 years on, includes over 500 titles,
from Arabic and Beekeeping to Yoga and Zulu.
What would you like to learn?

be where you want to be with **teach yourself**

For UK order enquiries: please contact Bookpoint Ltd, 130 Milton Park, Abingdon, Oxon OX14 4SB. Telephone: +44 (0) 1235 827720. Fax: +44 (0) 1235 400454. Lines are open 09.00–17.00, Monday to Saturday, with a 24-hour message answering service. Details about our titles and how to order are available at www.teachyourself.co.uk

For USA order enquiries: please contact McGraw-Hill Customer Services, PO Box 545, Blacklick, OH 43004-0545, USA. Telephone: 1-800-722-4726. Fax: 1-614-755-5645.

For Canada order enquiries: please contact McGraw-Hill Ryerson Ltd, 300 Water St, Whitby, Ontario L1N 9B6, Canada. Telephone: 905 430 5000. Fax: 905 430 5020.

Long renowned as the authoritative source for self-guided learning – with more than 50 million copies sold worldwide – the **teach yourself** series includes over 500 titles in the fields of languages, crafts, hobbies, business, computing and education.

British Library Cataloguing in Publication Data: a catalogue record for this title is available from the British Library.

Library of Congress Catalog Card Number: on file.

First published in UK 2009 by Hodder Education, part of Hachette UK, 338 Euston Road, London, NW1 3BH.

First published in US 2009 by The McGraw-Hill Companies, Inc.

This edition published 2009.

The **teach yourself** name is a registered trade mark of Hodder Headline.

Copyright © 2009 Dee Reid and Diana Bentley

Typeset by Transet Limited, Coventry, England.
Printed in Great Britain for Hodder Education, an Hachette UK Company, 338 Euston Road, London NW1 3BH, by CPI Cox & Wyman, Reading, Berkshire RG1 8EX.

The publisher has used its best endeavours to ensure that the URLs for external websites referred to in this book are correct and active at the time of going to press. However, the publisher and the author have no responsibility for the websites and can make no guarantee that a site will remain live or that the content will remain relevant, decent or appropriate.

Hachette UK's policy is to use papers that are natural, renewable and recyclable products and made from wood grown in sustainable forests. The logging and manufacturing processes are expected to conform to the environmental regulations of the country of origin.

Impression number   10 9 8 7 6 5 4 3 2 1
Year   2012 2011 2010 2009

contents

acknowledgements

Our thanks go to all those parents and children who have helped us with this book.

In particular we would like to thank:

Nancy and Bethan
Fauz, Claire and Issa
Katie and Jake
Rachel, Joseph and Hannah
Rachel and Grace

Also we are very grateful to those parents who sent us so many excellent questions (and waited so patiently for the answers!).

introduction

Children are in school for only 9 minutes of every waking hour between birth and 16 years. The other 51 minutes are spent in the home and the community.

Tim Brighouse, *The Times Educational Supplement* (2 April 1999)

Scientists tell us that about one half of an adult's intelligence is developed by the age of four, so the parental role in a child's intellectual development cannot be underestimated. Indeed, researchers concluded that 'parental involvement in their child's literacy practices is a more powerful force than other family background variables, such as social class, family size and level of parental education' (Flouri and Buchanan, 2004).

Children who start school having heard and used thousands of words (and who understand what those words mean) will have a distinct advantage. As the academic Maryanne Wolf says, in her intriguingly entitled study 'Proust and the Squid': 'Children who never have a story read to them, who never hear words that rhyme, who never imagine fighting with dragons or marrying a prince, have the odds overwhelmingly against them.'

Research into how children learn to read is the most investigated area of education. However, despite all this professional expertise, we cannot say for certain exactly how a child learns (or does not learn) to read. This is because reading is such a complex skill and all children are individuals and learn in different ways.

If you have picked up this book then you are already thinking about how to best help your child with reading. There is so much that parents can do to help but many parents do not know the best ways to go about it.

Everybody wants the best for their child but this eagerness can so easily tip over into becoming unrealistic expectations of what their child can do. The challenge facing parents is to strike a balance between active support (which is very valuable to a child's learning) and over-anxious pressure (which can be so damaging).

This book gives clear guidance to parents on when and how to support their child's learning and when to ease off and celebrate what their child can already do.

In this book you will learn:

- how talking to your child is the foundation for your child becoming a reader
- how reading to even very small babies will develop their speech and language
- how to read to your children of all ages
- how to help your child to make a successful start with reading
- how schools teach reading
- how to support your child once she has learned to read
- how to help your child if she has reading difficulties.

All parents want their children to become happy and confident readers as effortlessly as possible. This book has been written to give you practical advice on how best to achieve this. Some children seem to acquire the skill of reading with surprising ease while others meet hurdles along the way. It is important to remember that there is not just one route to becoming a reader. Parents who are seeing a second child through the stages of learning to read will know that each child goes along that route at their own pace and according to their own personality.

How to use this book

This book has been designed to be a simple step-by-step guide to enable parents to support their child learning to read.

Each chapter is devoted to a different step along the journey from 0 months to 11 years of age. It is not expected that you will read the book from beginning to end but rather that you will select the chapters that are relevant to you and your child. For practical purposes the chapters are titled with a specific age range, for example, 0–12 months; 5–7 years. However, children's development is not predictable. Every child develops uniquely. This means that it is sensible to read the chapter before and the chapter after the one devoted specifically to your child's age. This will give you a greater context for the advice on offer. Reading the chapter before will give you relevant background, describing milestones your child may have passed. Reading the chapter beyond will give you goals for you and your child to achieve. Regardless of your child's age, every parent should read Chapter 01, 'How to read to your child'.

Chapters 02–10 have:

- a brief introduction to the theory
- practical tips to try at home
- suggestions for making the most of the home-school partnership
- ideas for making reading fun
- interesting case studies
- frequently asked questions.

Lots of parents are concerned that they might do more harm than good when it comes to helping their child to read. Don't worry! This book will reassure you and give you plenty of sound advice that is easy to put into practice. We cannot guarantee that your child will have an effortless journey into reading but this book provides guidance that will give you the confidence to enjoy that journey together.

Please note that the male and female pronouns have been alternated in each chapter of this book. This is for convenience only and not because the focus of each chapter is necessarily gender specific.

01

how to read to your child (0–11 years)

In this chapter you will learn:
- simple tips to make reading aloud fun for you and your child
- how to dramatize readings to make them come alive
- how to arouse your child's curiosity in words
- how reading aloud expressively helps your child acquire new language.

Of all the pre-school experiences examined, being read aloud to by a parent was the one most strongly associated with reading achievement at age seven and again at school leaving age. It appeared to be the most powerful predictor of success.

Gordon Wells, *The Meaning Makers* (1985)

Reading is not the same as reading aloud

Most adults might assume that because they are good at reading they are good at reading aloud. They would be wrong! Reading aloud is a special skill. It's not difficult to learn how to do it well but if you want your children to really enjoy your book sharing sessions (and you want to compete with visually stimulating children's TV) then it is worth putting in a bit of effort to become good at reading aloud.

Why read aloud?

You may have tangible wealth untold:
Caskets of jewels and coffers of gold.
Richer than I you can never be –
I had a mother who read to me.

From 'The Reading Mother' by Strickland Gillilan (1936)

Reading aloud to your child lays down the foundation for his future success with literacy:

Reading aloud to your baby helps him to tune into the patterns of language. It provides a model for him when he begins to explore spoken language.

Reading aloud to your toddler provides him with a breadth of language experience that it is not possible to introduce through everyday spoken language. It also teaches him about the music of language and the excitement of the sound of words.

Reading aloud to your pre-school child helps him to distinguish separate words from the stream of spoken language. This is vital as he develops an interest in the printed form of language – the word. Hearing the same story over and over again gives your child the security of knowing what happens next in a story. He will be able to join in with your reading before he can recognize the words on the page.

Reading aloud to your five- to seven-year-old year old provides the perfect backdrop to his own developing reading skills. It becomes the incentive for him to persevere with the skills of reading as he has the goal of being able to read for himself the books you have shared with him.

Reading aloud to older children is what keeps them engaged in the act of reading. They might be able to read for themselves but if you read aloud to them it can be a bonding experience between a parent and child. It demonstrates that you are willing to spend time together enjoying books.

How to read aloud

Spending time reading aloud to your child, whatever his age, will be beneficial for all sorts of reasons but if you put in a little effort to become good at reading aloud you will maximize the benefits. Most parents have had very little experience of reading aloud to anyone since they were seven years of age! Most would benefit from a refresher course.

Ten tips when reading aloud

1 Don't read too quickly

It might sound an obvious thing to say but some adults adopt a reading aloud pace which is close to their normal silent reading pace. When we read silently we are able to skim along the line of print very swiftly and yet we can still retain the meaning of what we are reading. But for the child listening to the reading and having to follow the meaning just by hearing the words, it is important that we read more slowly, allowing the words and phrases to fall upon the child's ears and then be absorbed by his mind.

2 Be dramatic

Aim to give as lively a reading as possible. Convey the drama of the story through your voice. If there is a sad part of the narrative, then let that come through in your voice. Don't be embarrassed! You may not pass an audition for RADA but your child will think you are the best performer in the world if you bring his books to life through your reading.

3 Be prepared

The best way to give an animated reading is to know what is coming next! When reading picture books to a younger child you could skim read the book before sharing it with your child. That way you know what is coming next and can make the most of the highs and lows of the tale.

Top tip

Don't panic if you do not always have time to prepare the book before you share it with your child. Chances are he will request the book again and again so even if your first reading is not an Oscar-winning performance then you will have plenty of opportunities to improve!

4 Try different voices

Try to put on different voices for different characters. Don't be too ambitious – it might be enough to have a deep growly voice for the bear or a squeaky voice for the mouse and then any other characters can be in your everyday speaking voice.

5 Keep the tension going

If there is a dramatic moment at the end of a right-hand page do not turn the page over too quickly. Savour the moment with your child. Behave as if you do not know (or haven't guessed) what is coming next. For example, say to your child: 'Oh no! Teddy has been thrown in the bin by mistake. Now he's lost forever!' Your child will enjoy the awfulness of contemplating teddy's demise (particularly if he knows from a previous reading that Teddy is found safe and well and is restored to his family).

6 Add in sound effects where appropriate

Lots of children's stories have animals in them so have a go at being an owl or add a moo when the cow appears. You could extend this to make verbs in the text more dramatic – if the crocodile snaps his jaws closed then you do the same and if a spooky ghost appears enjoy a lot of 'ooooow' sounds!

7 Stress some words

When you are reading imagine some words are in bold and give these words extra emphasis. For example, when Daddy Bear sees that someone has been eating his porridge, say in a big growly voice: 'Who's been eating **my** porridge?'

8   Let your child join in

If you are reading an old favourite then pause before a significant word and let your child have the pleasure of joining in.

> **Top tip**
>
> If your child is aged four or over then gently point at the word you have left him to say. That way he is saying a word he already knows but you have drawn attention to the printed form of that word. He will begin to make the important link between words he hears and can say and words he can see.

9   Give your child time to enjoy the pictures

Don't forget that while you may be following the printed words your child's gaze will be on the pictures. The artwork in picture books is not just illustrating the text, often there is a wealth of detail in the pictures that is not alluded to in the text. Help your child to study the pictures to enjoy all the extras that a gifted illustrator has brought to the book.

10 Stop if your child seems bored

Accept the fact that sometimes, despite your skilled performance, your child might just not be in the mood. Never insist that he listens if he seems reluctant. Put the book away and choose another activity together. Don't walk away as that is telling your child that if he is not prepared to listen to your reading then you are not prepared to spend time with him. After a few minutes of quiet play together you could offer to read to him again. He might be ready to share a book with you but if not, then leave it for another day.

Reading aloud to your baby (0–12 months)

You can start reading aloud to your baby as soon there are any gaps between feeding him and him falling asleep! Choose a short book of about eight pages in length which repeats a phrase or sentence on each page, for example, a book called 'Baby's Day' might go something like this: 'First ... a sleepy baby, then a hungry baby, then a bouncing baby, then a smiling baby, then a happy baby and ... then a sleepy baby again.' Of course, your baby won't be looking at the book but he will hear the same patterns of words spoken each time and the gentle sound of this repeated language will not only be very comforting to him but it will be tuning his ears to the significant sounds of spoken language.

Top tip

If you or your partner is bilingual, this very first experience with books is an ideal time for your baby to hear the different sounds made by another language. Read to your baby in both languages and his ears will begin to distinguish the different patterns of sounds.

Make your voice convey the meaning

As your baby begins to spend more time awake, you can cradle him in your arms and hold a simple board book for him to see. Don't worry if your baby does not focus on the pages as you turn them. He will eventually learn to look where you are looking. Even at this very beginning stage of reading aloud you can make the most of how you say the words. So, using the example above, say each adjective in a way that conveys its meaning: a 'sleepy' baby – dwell on the word 'sleepy' and bring out its two syllables. Sound drowsy in the way you pronounce it. Then say each of the other adjectives in ways that emphasize their meanings, for example, sound a little desperate in your pronunciation of the word 'hungry' as if you were a baby getting a bit anxious that your dinner was not being produced quickly enough and when you come to 'a bouncing baby' make your voice sound light and bouncy (and maybe add a little bouncing action).

Top tip

You do not need lots of different books at this stage. A small number of books that have just a few pages and a similar phrase on each page will be sufficient.

Should I use books with just one word on a page?

While your baby is very young and before he begins to focus on the pages of a book, it is better to use books which have a phrase on each page and not just a single word, for example, 'sleeping', 'hungry', 'smiling', etc. At this early stage it is best for your baby to hear a phrase of language which is more melodious than speaking a single word. Later on when your baby can look at a page and follow your finger as you point at the object on the page then books which name objects are great but for now your goal is to immerse your baby in the sweetest music to his ears – the sound of your voice!

Reading aloud to your toddler (1–3 years)

Toddlers are hungry for information and some of the books you read to them at this stage will name things in the world around them; things that are familiar such as chair, teddy, cot, bottle, and things that are exotic such as tiger, digger, train. Your toddler is beginning to notice things in great detail and he will study the pictures in these books with some concentration.

Adding dialogue to your reading

Just because the book has only one word per page does not mean you need to restrict yourself to just reading the one word in a robotic style. It is important that your toddler begins to associate the name of the object with its picture but you are not drilling him for some later vocabulary test! Say the name of the object clearly and with interest but then make some association between the object and your toddler. For example, if there is a picture of a baby's drinking mug on a page, your book talk might go something like this:

Mug – 'Look at this nice blue mug. Can you see the handles? There are two handles' – (point at each in turn and count, one, two). 'I wonder what is in the mug. Could it be milk? Could it be juice? Is your mug blue?' (Wait for your toddler to reply but do not expect him necessarily to do so.) Then answer your own question: 'No, your mug isn't blue is it? You have got a lovely yellow mug haven't you? And what do you like best in your lovely yellow mug? You like milk, don't you?'

It is not essential that you follow exactly the same script each time but your purpose at this stage is to extend your toddler's vocabulary and to relate the picture to things that are meaningful in his world.

Books with more text

Of course, as your baby moves through the toddler stage you will not want to restrict your sharing of books to books that name things. You will also be sharing books with a simple narrative. These books may not need as many additional comments from you as the 'word books' but you should still relate what you are reading to your toddler to your own lives. So if the book you are reading is about a visit to see Granny but you and your toddler call your mother (or your partner's mother) 'Gran' (or Nan, Nanny, Grandma or anything else) then change the word in the book to the word that means most to your toddler.

Books with more text will give your toddler exposure to the pattern of complete sentences which spoken language does not. Tuning in to how sentences make meaning of language is the best preparation for becoming a reader and writer.

Ask questions

It is a good idea to ask questions as you read aloud to your toddler. The questions are not to check up on your toddler's comprehension but rather to make the reading experience relate to your own lives. So if you are reading about a sleeping bear in a cave you could ask your toddler, 'Would you go into the cave?' It is perfectly all right to then answer your own question: 'I think the bear looks very friendly and I think I would go into the cave to give him a stroke on his soft fur.' Your toddler will come to understand the nature of questions (indicated by the way your voice rises at the end of the sentence) and also come to realize that a question needs an answer. This exchange of dialogue will help your toddler understand the rules of conversation and even though the conversation will be fairly one-sided at the beginning, the pattern of asking a question and waiting for a reply (before you supply it) will be a tune of language your toddler will quickly pick up and before too long he will be able to give an answer of his own.

Reading aloud to your pre-school child (3–4 years)

As your child grows, his stamina for reading aloud sessions will increase but there will also be lots of other competition for his attention and interest so it is important that your reading aloud to him is not just something you do in the hope of pacifying him before bedtime. Your book sharing sessions could take place at any time of the day – after breakfast, before lunch or even during tea! These sessions need to be as exciting and engaging as any other entertainment he may have available. Your goal is to read aloud with as much expression as you can and to encourage your child to join in as you read.

Joining in

As your child's vocabulary expands he will enjoy joining in when you read to him. Of course, your child will only be able to do this if you have read the story a good few times and then given him a big cue to indicate when he comes in with 'his' word or words. So, for example, if you were reading the beginning of the traditional tale, 'Goldilocks and the Three Bears' and you have read 'Once upon a time there were three bears. There was great big Daddy bear. There was middle-sized Mummy bear and there was ...' you could draw out the word 'was' and then stop and there is every chance that your child will come in on cue with 'little Baby bear'. Your child will be thrilled at making this contribution to the story and he is also learning about how language works and how we use expression in our voices for effect. The expression that you use is one of the ways that helps children to remember what comes next and they will try to say the missing words in the same way as you have previously read them.

Questions and discussion

The questioning technique which you started when your child was a toddler should be continued at this stage too, but now you can ask genuine questions as well as the rhetorical questions used at the earlier stage. So, for example, when looking at an information book about cars, you could ask your child: 'Who do we know who has a car like that?' These questions should run alongside your other questions which are also your means of ensuring that your child fully understands the text. For example, after you have just read about the maximum speed of a particular car, you might say (almost in a tone of disbelief) 'How fast is that?'

The pointing finger

At this stage you can also begin to use your finger to point at words as you say them. You do not need to stab at each word and then say it: that takes away so much of the pleasure your child will have enjoyed in your read aloud sessions and turns it into some kind of drill or exercise. Rather, you should allow your finger to casually point at a word just as you are about to say it. You might like to combine this with the technique of giving your child space to join in as you read, so that there are some words in the text which you cue for him by reading up to the word with expression, but then you hold back and allow your child to say the remembered word. If, at that same moment, your finger is unobtrusively pointing at that very word, you are helping your child to associate the sound of a word with the look of the word. This association of known spoken words with their written versions is the beginning of a child understanding about how writing is spoken language written down.

> **Top tip**
>
> Don't get too carried away with this technique and turn it into a test! If your child is not enjoying being the one who says the 'missing' word then ease off from this approach for a week or two before trying the procedure again. Some children sense very quickly if you are turning the pleasure of a shared reading experience into a lesson and they may resent the change!

Reading aloud to your 4–7-year-old

Should you stop reading aloud to your child once he starts school? Absolutely not! As he begins the more formal aspects of learning to read and write the ideal preparation for this is a steady diet of books read and shared together at home. Ask any teacher what they would do if they had more time in the school day and they would say that they would spend more time reading aloud to the class. In the pressure of a busy school day there is only so much time that a teacher can spend immersing children in the magical world and language of books. But parents have that time – even busy parents who work long hours can make time to share books with their children. Learning to read is a challenge, but those children who are familiar with the pleasure of books generally make the smoothest progression into becoming readers.

How does sharing books with my child fit in with 'hearing him read'?

Once children start formal schooling it is usual for schools to send a reading scheme book home with each child for them to practise the skills of reading that they have been learning in the classroom. These books usually have a simple, repeated text using words your child can recognize or decode (blend the sounds of the letters to read the words). The more practice your child has, the more speedily he will recognize the words. However, recognizing words is only part of the skill of reading. To successfully read a text we need also to understand what we have read. Just as you elaborated the simple text of the board book to make it meaningful for your toddler when he was younger, so you should expand the reading scheme text to give the context to the simple repeated language. So the text your child reads might only be: 'Is the ball in here?', 'No, it is not.' 'Is the ball in here?', 'Yes, it is.' But you can bring it alive for your child through talk. For example, 'Oh look, the puppy is looking for his favourite ball. Where is he looking? That's right, he's looking in the cupboard.' (Now point at the words for your child to read: 'Is the ball in here?') Then continue your conversation with your child: 'Is the ball in the cupboard?' and this will prompt him to read: 'No, it is not.'

Reading to your child as well as hearing him read

Just because your child is beginning to develop some independent reading skills is not an indication that you should stop reading to him. Reading aloud favourite stories and information books will be the incentive your child needs to persevere with the skills of reading so that he can enjoy those treats for himself later on. By continuing to read aloud to your child you are demonstrating the status that you place on sharing books together.

Print makes sense

Children who have been read to from their earliest days will grow up with the expectation that print makes sense. When children start reading the simple text in the books from school which are designed to teach reading, they will often stumble over words and say the wrong word. For example, they may confuse the word 'go' with 'do'. The child who is familiar with hearing stories read and shared with them will realize that only one of these words makes sense in the context and so they will go back and correct the word that does not make sense. This strong urgency to make sense of what they are reading is an invaluable skill when learning to read and the drive to make sense of a text comes from the experience of being read to.

Word games

When your child was younger you used your finger to 'land' on an interesting word just as you said it. Now your child is learning to read and to focus on the print as well as the pictures, you can support his learning by pointing at words he might recognize on his own. The best way to do this is by playing games. After you have read and enjoyed one of his favourite stories, you might re-visit one or two pages of the book to encourage him to look more purposely at some of the words. For example, you might say: 'Can you find the word "the" two times on this page?' or 'I bet I can point at the word "and" quicker than you can.' Remember that this is a game and not a test and if your child doesn't enjoy showing off his word (or letter) knowledge then quit and just spend your time reading to him.

Following the print

Another way to share books with the emergent reader is for you to gently run your finger along the line of print as you read it. You are not emphasizing each word as you say it but you are demonstrating how in English orthography, print is read from left to right.

Texts first, then words and letter sounds

The best way for children to learn the relationship between words, letters and sounds is to be introduced to them in the following order:

- First concentrate on the whole text (story or information), which engages your child and entertains him.
- Then draw your child's attention to particular words either because they are fun words to say like 'ferocious' or because they are words that have occurred in his reading book from school (such as 'can' or 'see').
- Next, look in more detail at those particular words. What letter do they have at the beginning? Do they rhyme with another word on the page?

So the sequence is from text to word to letter to sound and not the other way round!

Should I avoid books with 'difficult' vocabulary?

Definitely not! Just because your child is only able to read 'simple' words in their school reading book does not mean you should limit your reading to him to the same restricted vocabulary. The children's author, Philip Pullman, said: 'When it comes to telling children stories they don't need simple language. They need beautiful language.' Exciting stories, and fascinating information books with a rich and varied range of language are the perfect counterpoint to the simpler text your child can manage independently.

Reading aloud to older children (7–11 years)

Many parents discover that once their child has learned to read, their pleasure in reading declines. This might seem contradictory as the whole purpose of reading to them and supporting their skills of learning to read has been that they are then able to read independently. So why might the child's enthusiasm for the task evaporate at the very time when they have achieved the goal of independent reading? Well, one answer might be that children between the ages of seven and 11 have many activities competing for their time – learning to swim, dance, play a musical instrument, going to gym club or karate club, playing football, rugby, tennis or cricket. So reading has to fit in between all these other activities. Also, once your child has acquired independent reading skills the 'necessity' of reading aloud to him declines. However, it would seem that those families who manage to sustain the habit of reading aloud together all through the pre-teen years are more likely to have children who not only can read but who actually choose to read. Most adults enjoy listening to a story on a CD or on the radio. They could have read that story in a book themselves but hearing it well read to them is a particularly enjoyable activity. By spending time reading aloud to your child long after he can read independently you are demonstrating the importance you place on the skill of reading. You are also conveying your enthusiasm for reading and, like so many things with child-rearing, the best lessons are those that are based on 'do as I do' rather than just 'do as I say'.

Frequently asked questions

My little boy is nearly four. He is beginning to be curious about letters and words. He can pick out some of the letters in his name. Now that he understands that I am reading the words printed on the page, should I point at the words as I read them?

It is great that your son is showing an interest in the print as well as the pictures. However, if you always point at the words as you read them, this will alter the speed and expression that you use when sharing a book with him. It might also change the pattern of your book sharing sessions from one of complete enjoyment on your son's part to one where he might feel he has to 'do' something, i.e. look closely at the different words. This might actually distract him from the sense of the words and phrases as you read them, which at this stage is the first priority. Later on, when your son is starting to read and you are sharing books designed to support the beginning stages of reading, then it can be a very good idea to support his reading by pointing at each word in turn. For further advice on this stage, see Chapter 07, page 152.

I quite liked reading to my daughter before she started school but now that she is eight and can read quite well for herself, I don't see much point in spending time reading to her.

It is worth persevering with reading aloud to your daughter even though she is making good progress as a reader herself. When you read to her you are able to choose books that she would not manage to read on her own. This means you are enticing her into the pleasures of more advanced books, which will encourage her to continue to enjoy reading. Many parents are tempted to give up on reading aloud to their children when their offspring can read independently but it is precisely at this stage that children benefit from the interest and enthusiasm of an adult reader. It is worth asking the librarian for advice on books suitable for you to read aloud to your daughter. Also you might like to ring the changes by borrowing story CDs for your daughter to listen to.

My husband is quite keen to do his share of reading to our six-year-old son but our son prefers me to read to him! I think it is because my husband is inclined to read too quickly and my son can't follow the story and doesn't have time to pore over the pictures. How can I slow my husband down?!

Lots of adults are unsure how to read aloud successfully to children. Quite naturally they adopt the reading pace they would use for their own reading or reading at work where there is an expectation that good readers will read quickly! In this chapter we have given advice on finding a suitable pace for reading and making each reading session a dramatic event. The main message is that reading quite slowly and savouring the words will ensure that your child understands what he is hearing and he is much more likely to adopt some of the vocabulary of the books into his own speech patterns if the words have been individually enjoyed. Reading at a slower pace might seem unnatural at first but once your husband is rewarded with the enjoyment your son gets from each reading session he will learn to adopt a reading pace that suits the story and your son.

Summary

The first priority of reading aloud to children is to delight and entertain them. It is not to teach them to read and it is often the children who have been read to most frequently that become the avid readers and writers. The greatest advantage of reading aloud to children is that it forms a strong connection in their minds between reading and pleasure and that is what will sustain them as they move forward into becoming independent readers.

Making the most of reading aloud

The following chart is a guide to how you might read aloud the first few pages of one particular picture book, *Mr. Gumpy's Outing*.

Text in the book	How you might read it
This is Mr. Gumpy.	Start slowly and steadily and slightly pause between each word to give it emphasis.
	Talk about Mr. Gumpy standing in his garden holding his watering can.
Mr. Gumpy owned a boat and his house was by a river.	Continue reading slowly and steadily with a slight emphasis on each noun: boat, house, river.
	Talk about the boat (which is a kind of punt) and the long pole that Mr. Gumpy uses to push the boat along.
One day Mr. Gumpy went out in his boat.	Now you are getting into the story proper so build in a bit of expectation in the way you say 'One day' with slightly more emphasis on the word 'One'.
'May we come with you?' said the children.	Use a suitable voice for the children and let your voice convey the request and longing in the children's voices.
'Yes,' said Mr. Gumpy,	Pause for a second before giving Mr. Gumpy's reply as if you were Mr. Gumpy giving the matter some consideration. Then dwell on the word 'Yes' almost making it two syllables with the second syllable slightly lower in tone.
'if you don't squabble.'	In this line make the most of the word 'squabble'. It's a lovely onomatopoeic word and each time in the book

the different animals request to come on Mr. Gumpy's boat he has a different proviso and by emphasizing this one you are setting up a pattern for how the other pages will be read.

First talk about the children in the boat and Mr. Gumpy steadily pushing on the pole to move the boat through the water.

'Can I come along, Mr. Gumpy?' said the rabbit.

Now introduce rabbit with a 'rabbity' voice. Maybe twitch your nose a little as you convey rabbit's eagerness to come on the boat.

'Yes, but don't hop about.'

You have got your pattern now for Mr. Gumpy's response – dwell on the 'Yes' and then make the most of the word 'hop'.

Before you turn the page you could ask your child if he thinks the rabbit will 'hop about'. You can ask this question even if your child has heard the story before and knows full well that is exactly what the rabbit does!

'I'd like a ride,' said the cat.

Now your task is to convey the supercilious nature of cats! So in an airily disdainful voice say the words of the cat.

'Very well,' said Mr. Gumpy, 'but you're not to chase the rabbit.'

Once again, Mr. Gumpy only agrees after some consideration, so say the words 'Very well,' quite slowly but make the terms and conditions very clear by emphasizing the word 'not'.

	Ask your child whether he thinks the cat will chase the rabbit.
'Will you take me with you?' said the dog.	Now you are the dog wanting to go on the boat and like all dogs you are eager to please so convey that in the way you make the request.
'Yes,' said Mr. Gumpy.	Continue with your pattern of how to read this line.
'But don't tease the cat.'	Now you can emphasize the words 'don't' and 'tease' and imply that you know the dog has done this before but this time you are trusting him to behave better!
	Ask your child whether he thinks the dog will tease the cat.
'May I come, please, Mr. Gumpy?' said the pig.	Put on a wheedling tone for the pig's request.
'Very well, but don't muck about.'	This will follow the pattern of how Mr. Gumpy responded to the cat and you will need to emphasize the words 'muck about' (which your child is likely to find highly amusing!).

Reading aloud techniques

Different voices for different characters

This is fairly obvious but if you can convey the worried character or the cheeky character (human or animal) in the way you say the words then you are also helping your child to understand the words he hears.

Words in capitals

Give these words plenty of emphasis. When reading a familiar story which has a word in capitals, pause just before you say the word loudly. Your child will love the moment of expectation just before the loud voice.

Use the speech verbs

If the speech verb suggests how a character speaks try to bring that into your reading so if the text is 'laughed the little dog' then bring a little chuckle into your voice. Or if the text says 'growled old bear' then try to make a growl come through in the way you say the word.

Add in actions whenever possible

If the text has a sleepy cat stretching out on the mat then 'stretch' the word as you say it and move your shoulder to indicate a lazy stretch. If one character gives another character a big hug then make sure you give your child a big hug too!

Top tip

Slow down! Savour every word. This will make each reading aloud session a joy for your child but it will also help to develop his vocabulary and understanding of each word.

What you have learned in this chapter

- Reading aloud to your child is beneficial whatever his age.
- If you make the most of each reading aloud session, your child will enjoy it all the more and gain the most from this time.
- Everyone can be good at reading aloud; it's just a case of practising a few techniques and finding your acting style to bring the text alive for your child.

02

reading and your baby (0–12 months)

In this chapter you will learn:
- how to share songs, rhymes and rhythms with your baby
- why you should read to your baby
- how to read to your baby
- what kind of books to share with your baby.

What a child can do in cooperation today, he or she can do alone tomorrow.

L. S. Vygotsky, *Thought and Language: The Zone of Proximal Development* (1962)

Laying down the foundations for literacy

Literacy begins at birth. From the moment you hold your baby in your arms and talk to her you are embarking upon the wonderful journey to literacy. When you greet your baby in the morning and she responds to your voice with a smile, she is learning that your face and the sound of your voice are safe and comforting. Soon your baby will come to recognize your voice and turn her head when you speak to her. Some people think that because she is too little to understand what you are saying there is no value in talking to her. They couldn't be more wrong! Long before she can understand what you are saying she is engaging with the sound of your voice and revelling in the comfort that it brings. This very early tuning in to spoken language is the foundation of later literacy. Language is the way we learn about ourselves and the world around us.

Talking to your baby

Try to make a habit of talking to your baby throughout the day by giving a running commentary on what you are doing and what is happening to her. You can use familiar phrases, such as 'Now we're going to the shops' or 'Let's have some dinner now.' With constant exposure to these familiar phrases children begin to associate what they hear with what they do. Then they begin to pick out words from your monologue – 'shops', 'dinner – yum, yum!' This is an easy and relaxed way to introduce your baby to the purpose and sound of spoken language.

Some people might feel a little embarrassed talking to a baby who cannot answer but the more you do it, the more natural it will become and, more importantly, you will be creating the best environment for language development.

Asking questions

As your baby approaches nine months of age you can begin to ask lots of questions: 'Shall we pop down to the shops to get some milk?' The trick is to wait for an answer (although your baby may not oblige you with an answer!) but she is learning how the sound of communication goes: one person speaks and another answers. This 'tune' of the give and take of conversation will be in place before she has words to make her answers.

Talking through the day

Case study: Bethan aged three months

At long last Bethan has dropped the 2.00 a.m. feed so when she wakes at around 6.00 a.m. she is hungry and ready to start her day. Her mother would go into Bethan's room saying 'Who's making all that noise? Someone must be very hungry and possibly a little bit wet too!' Then Bethan's mum would change her nappy chatting all the time.

After a feed, Bethan's mum would sing her a nursery rhyme or a little jingle. Then Bethan's mum would put her in the bouncing cradle as she got dressed explaining what she was going to wear saying, 'Now it's a bit chilly this morning so I'm going to wear this nice soft brown jumper. Mmmmmm! Feel how soft it is.' Bethan's mum would continue in this way surrounding Bethan in a rich diet of language.

Of course, each day will bring situations which will require different language – new things to see and talk about – but many of the daily routines, such as on first waking, after a feed or when changing and dressing your baby, present the opportunity to use the same phrases to accompany the actions. For example, 'Let's put on a nice clean nappy and then you will be the sweetest smelling baby in the world.'

What is Bethan learning?

She is learning:

- that comforting sounds of speech accompany her daily routine

- that she is the focus of her mother's attention
- that some sounds of speech will signify that pleasant things are going to happen, for example, she will be picked up and cuddled.

The role of the caring adult who surrounds the baby with tender talk can, of course, be undertaken by professionals in the nursery or day care setting. What is important is that the talk is going on, not who is doing the talk.

Songs, rhymes and rhythms

Apart from chatting away to accompany every part of your baby's day, babies also need the strong repetition and rhythmic beat of songs and rhymes.

Some people might be embarrassed at singing to their baby but remember you are not auditioning for a Lloyd Webber musical and your baby is not a strict judge on a Pop Idol programme! You don't have to be a good singer to entertain your baby. She will love any attempts you make to sing to her.

The repetition and rhythm in songs and rhymes allow babies to tune in to language in a slightly different way from the conversational language with which you surround your baby. Hearing the words of a song set in a melody over and over again is a perfect way to immerse her in the world of language.

Just as your baby will not understand all the language you use to accompany her day, so it doesn't matter if the words of the rhyme don't make perfect sense. Many nursery rhymes are based on historical figures or political events, the significance of which are long lost but the rhyme continues with its mesmerizing language and tune. The rhyme 'Ring a Ring O' Roses' refers to the time when the Black Death raged across Europe in the fourteenth century. Not a particularly cheerful theme to share with a young baby! But the rhyme, alliteration and tune will captivate your baby if you sing it again and again as you rock her in your arms.

Sharing songs and rhymes with your baby is the ideal opportunity for the bilingual parent to introduce the rhythms and cadences of their own language.

Case study: Issa aged four months

Fauz is from Kenya and married to Claire, a Londoner. They have a four-month-old boy called Issa. Right from the start, Fauz chose to speak to Issa in Swahili. As he rocks Issa to sleep he sings the lullabies his mother sang to him on the island of Lamu. Claire uses English when she talks to Issa and she sings English nursery rhymes, old and new to him. So Issa is hearing two languages and this exposure to two sets of speech sounds is enriching his language experience as well as creating a close bond with the language of both parents.

Top tip

If your memory of nursery rhymes is a bit hazy then it is a good idea to invest in an anthology of nursery rhymes. If your memory of the tunes of the rhymes needs a brush up then there are many excellent CDs of nursery rhymes available from libraries, bookshops, supermarkets and the web.

Sharing a book with your baby (0–5 months)

Just as it is never too soon to surround your baby with talk, so it is never too soon to share a book with her. (For guidance on what kind of books to share with young babies see page 26.) You certainly do not need to wait until your baby is able to talk before you start enjoying books together. Even very tiny babies will engage with the pleasure of hearing your voice and looking at the bright simple pictures. While they may not be able to consistently focus on a picture all the time, babies do have moments of focus and your enthusiastic sharing of the pictures will attract their attention: 'Ooooh! I can see a little teddy. And … here is another teddy.' Your baby will be drawn to the music of your voice speaking with expression.

Another enjoyable way to share books is to snuggle up with your baby, either in a chair or in the bed, and to lull her to sleep with the sound of your voice. On other occasions you might like to place your baby on your lap so that she can see what you are reading and you could read aloud your favourite magazine. What you are doing in this situation is surrounding your baby with an experience of language that will sound different from the rhythms and sounds of language you use when you talk directly to her throughout the day (see 'Talking through the day' on page 22).

Any time spent sharing a book with your baby will create a sense of security and contentment. This will be a firm foundation for a future enjoyment of books.

Checklist

• Start now! It's never too soon to start sharing books with your baby.
• Add books to your cuddle and snuggle times.
• Surround-sound your baby with book talk.

Can my baby see the pictures in a book?

Contrary to previously held ideas, babies are able to focus at any age but they are not able to control this focus as adults can. This does not mean that a baby of two months can see everything clearly because the brain areas responsible for clear vision are not yet completely developed. Nevertheless, they are capable of enjoying a rich visual world. Also the speed at which the focusing ability develops is dramatic. By four months your baby's vision is twice as accurate as it was at two months. By eight months it is twice as good again and by 12 months it is as good as an adult's.

It was thought that giving babies the visual stimulus of black and white mobiles and toys would provide them with the best opportunity for seeing clearly. It is now known that babies can detect much subtler shades of grey and that by three months of age your baby can distinguish all of the range of colours they see around them.

Case study: Sam aged three months

When Sam was three months old his mother began to show him books. She would sit on the floor and prop him up between her knees. She had several small board books with simple photos of everyday objects in them. She would point at the pictures and talk about the object on the page. She said that very often he fell asleep and she wasn't sure if he went to sleep because he was bored or because he was peaceful and comfortable!

She tried to sit and look at a book with him each day but often there just did not seem to be enough time. After a few months she noticed that when she was showing him a book and pointing at each picture, he seemed to be following her finger with his eyes. Sometimes she would leave a page open for several minutes and he seemed glued to the picture.

What is Sam learning?

Sam is learning:

- that books are fun
- to listen as his mum reads to him
- that books have pictures
- that his mum likes sharing a book with him.

What kind of books should you share with your 0–5-month-old baby?

Very little babies need very soft books! Small but chunky fabric books make ideal first books to share. The pictures should be bright and clear and in primary colours. While babies can detect subtle colours, their eyes will be drawn to pictures where there is the greatest contrast between colours. There are many of these kinds of books available from websites, bookshops and supermarkets.

Look for books that have just one everyday object on each page, for example, a teddy or a bottle. Don't just use the single word to describe the picture, but try to embed the word in sentences, for example, 'Oh, look at the teddy. Teddy looks so soft and cuddly.' So long as you repeat the word 'teddy' in every sentence your baby will learn to associate that word when she sees that picture.

Some of these very simple books may have the word written below the object but at this early stage it is best to concentrate on pointing at the picture as your baby may be able to notice the colours of the picture but there is no point in drawing her attention to the printed word!

Checklist

- Choose soft books for inquisitive fingers.
- One picture per page is quite enough!
- Talk! Surround your baby with talk about the pictures.

Sharing a book with your baby (6–12 months)

The first books to share with your baby of six months plus will need to be durable! Now your baby will not be content with just looking at pictures, she will want to touch them and probably also chew them! For this reason, a sturdy board book makes a sensible choice for reading to her because your baby is able to get her small fingers between the thick pages and experiment with turning them.

Clever babies!

Most board books depict clear pictures of objects the baby is familiar with around the house like their bottle, mug, teddy, or a banana. At this stage babies make a huge leap in conceptual understanding. They become aware that something that they hold and eat can be presented in a two-dimensional drawing. Indeed, don't be surprised if, initially, your baby tries to pick up the picture of the bottle in the book as if it were a real object! The more you share books with your baby the more familiar she will become with the idea of pictorial representation. But that is not the only conceptual advance your baby has to make. She will also learn that we use the word 'teddy' to describe a picture of a teddy in the book even though it may not be identical to her own favourite teddy.

Don't expect this understanding of generalizing to happen immediately. It will take many sessions of book sharing for babies to acquire this level of comprehension. It is easy for us to underestimate what an achievement this is and the more time you spend reading books to your baby the swifter that understanding will be.

> **Top tip**
>
> A good way to have a book that is guaranteed to interest your baby is to take photographs of her familiar objects, for example, her bottle, her cot, her mug, her teddy. You could also add a picture of her granny, a picture of yourselves and finally a picture of herself. Pop these photos into an A5 slip-in album. It will be the most popular book around!

Broadening their horizons

Of course in any board book there will be pictures of objects that your baby may not be familiar with in real life. For example, the book may have a picture of a kitten. As your baby hears you use the word 'kitten' every time you come to that picture, then gradually she learns to associate that word with the picture of the kitten. If you use the same book many times then your child hears the same word for the same object and this knowledge becomes embedded into her 'hearing' vocabulary.

> **Top tip**
>
> In the bilingual home, where one parent may be using a different language with the baby, it is a good idea for each parent to name the objects in the board books in their own language. This will not muddle the young baby but tune them in to the richness of vocabulary in more than one language.

Interactive books

From about the age of six months your baby may begin to enjoy soft fabric books or small board books that have an interactive element such as lift-the-flap. She may be beginning to sustain an interest across a simple sequence of actions, for example, 'Is Teddy in here? No. Is Teddy in here? Yes.' It is important to remember that your baby will enjoy this kind of book all the more if you share it with her at an unhurried pace. Your baby will need time to focus on the page and time to reach out and lift the flap. Each time you share a book like this with your baby, treat it as if it were the first time so that it is always a surprise to discover where teddy is hiding. This pretence enhances your baby's involvement with the action and lays down the foundation for the pleasure that comes from knowing something but pretending not to know.

When reading books with a sentence on each page don't feel restricted to just saying the printed words. Engage your baby by commenting on the decision as you open each flap. For example, 'Now let's see if Teddy is hiding here.' Guide her fingers to the flap and help her to lift it open.

If your baby shows an interest in holding the book then encourage her to do so. Gradually she will attempt to turn the pages. Do not worry if her first attempts result in several pages being turned at once. Bit by bit your baby's dexterity will increase and she will be able to turn pages accurately.

Top tip

Don't feel that your baby must have a wide selection of books. It is valuable at this stage for your baby to become very familiar with a smaller range of books that she will treat as favourite toys.

Checklist

- Go at your baby's pace. You can remember what is behind the flap but it will be a while before she does.
- Let your baby experiment with page turning.
- Talk! Surround your baby with talk about the pictures.

Pictures or words?

Your baby is still too little to even notice the printed words that may be below the pictures of some of the books you share with her. This does not mean you need to avoid books with words, but there is no point in distracting her from the picture to draw her attention to the print. There is plenty of time for her to become curious about print later on (see Chapter 07).

What is my baby learning when we share books?

Apart from developing an understanding about how real objects can be represented pictorially and also developing a wider vocabulary, your baby is also learning how books 'work' and that:

- books open and shut
- books have different pictures on different pages
- you turn the pages to get to another picture
- you use a quiet and comforting voice when you are looking at the book or an exciting dramatic voice for emphasis
- it's nice to sit quietly, if only for a few moments, when you have a book in your hand
- she can turn the pages with help
- she likes books that have some interaction like flaps or touchy feely pages.

Case study: Aditya aged eight months

At eight months Aditya could sit up on her own. Her mum used to put toys around her and included a book so that she could grab that if she wished. Some days she saw her pick it up and open it, some days she saw her chew it!

At nine months Aditya was rolling over to get to things she wanted. She could get up onto her hands and knees but would not set off crawling despite her mum crawling around the floor trying to encourage her! Her mum noticed that Aditya did not seem so interested in books although she tried to share a book with her as often as possible. Then she bought a book with flaps to lift and this really sparked Aditya's enjoyment, especially when her mum pretended to be surprised when she lifted the flap to display the animal. This would make Aditya giggle and, after that, she began to try to manage the book on her own if it was left nearby.

What books to share with your baby (6–12 months)

The following books are all suitable to share with your baby:

- board books of all kinds
- cloth/fabric books

- lift-the-flap books with just words or a single line per page
- tactile books with pages to crinkle
- books with a toy tie-in, for example, Maisy Mouse™ or a Matchbox® book with a fire engine
- 'buggy books' complete with a clip to fasten to the buggy
- bath books
- home-made books: take photos of familiar objects and your baby and slip them into a slim A5 photo album
- 'tray play' books with a sucker on the back to hold them steady.

Top tip

Don't only share books just before you want to put your baby down for a sleep! She will quickly learn that book sharing is followed by her being left on his own and she may resent this! Share a book as often as you can during the day. Remember this activity need only last three to five minutes. The good news is that, for many babies, the quiet time and familiar activity of book sharing often does make them drowsy and ready for a little nap!

Sure Start

This is a UK initiative to support parents of children aged 0–14. Part of the Sure Start programme is Bookstart which provides free books for babies and young toddlers from birth until age four. (For more information see 'Taking it further' on page 228 or go to www.surestart.gov.uk) The Bookstart pack also includes a guide for parents choosing books for their babies called 'Babies Love Books'.

Baby signing

Wouldn't it be wonderful if your baby could let you know if she was hungry, thirsty or tired other than by crying? 'Baby signing' is a technique for teaching babies a few simple signs to convey their needs. In the UK it is based on the signs of British Sign Language (in the USA it is based on American Sign Language) and it is used by parents who can hear and who use signs to communicate with their hearing babies. Babies naturally use their arms to gesture and they are able to co-ordinate and control their hand muscles much earlier than their speech muscles. So the theory is that, by introducing babies to simple signs, we can help them to communicate their feelings from as young as eight months. This may reduce frustration of both parents and baby.

How did baby signing start?

Signing was first marketed in the USA by Dr Joseph Garcia of the University of Alaska who found that hearing babies communicated earlier with their deaf parents using sign language than hearing babies did with their hearing parents. He devised a simplified system of signing for hearing babies and this approach has become very popular both in the USA and in the UK.

What is baby signing?

The principle underlying baby signing is that you teach your baby to make an association between a sign and what it represents. For example, the sign for 'hot' is touching something and then pulling your hand away rapidly while saying 'hot'. The sign for 'milk' is to open and close the fingers of one hand. The idea is that by constantly using the same sign and the associated word, your baby will be able to make that sign and indicate her needs.

Should I baby sign?

There have been some concerns that baby signing may inhibit speech but this would only happen if signing were used in place of speech. Signs should be used in conjunction with speech to provide babies with a multi-sensory environment.

Whether all babies need the outlet of signing is debatable but the techniques involved in signing are good parent/baby procedures. In 2000, Drs Linda Acredolo and Susan Goodwyn of California University found that signing promotes excellent interaction because when signing, parents automatically adopt positive interaction strategies such as following the child's focus of interest, making eye contact, speaking slowly and repetitively, and using simple key words. Signing with babies under 12 months old is best kept for situations which elicit the particular vocabulary, so that the child is experiencing the situation when the sign is used accompanied by the word. There doesn't seem a lot of point in training them to sign for objects that are not immediate to their needs (such as the sign for butterfly) unless, perhaps, you are sharing a book about a butterfly.

The pleasure a parent experiences when a baby first smiles back at them is the incentive for both the parent and baby to recreate the situation. There is no doubt that if your young baby succeeds in communicating through a sign, your evident delight will be rewarding to both you and your baby.

Advocates of baby signing believe that it can strengthen the bond between babies and parents and that it could even help babies to learn to speak earlier than usual. However, other researchers suggest that training babies to communicate using signs may inhibit the natural development of other skills besides language. Learning to communicate is not the only skill your baby needs to acquire at this stage. There's a whole world out there she is learning to engage with: she is also learning to listen, socialize, move, feed herself, and develop manual dexterity. The jury is out on the claims that baby signing enhances a baby's verbal communication but there is no doubt that the time that a parent spends signing to their baby will reap benefits in terms of the baby's contentment and eagerness to communicate. Whether this benefit accrues from the signing process or simply from the time devoted to communication of any sort is difficult to say. For further information about baby signing see 'Taking it further', pages 230–1.

Parental angst

Parents today are under enormous pressure to perform well as parents. They can be made to feel guilty if they are not doing everything recommended by infancy specialists and the infancy industry (which is big business). Everyone wants the best for their offspring but don't feel pressurized into buying into a programme that may achieve no more than what you could do on your own, for free.

Top tip

If your baby loves the baby signing classes and you feel that it is helping you communicate with your baby and you enjoy the chance to meet other parents and get out of the house, then go for it, but don't forget your time might just as well be spent reading and talking to your baby!

TV and the young baby

Watching television is part of most adults' lives so it might seem natural that it should also be part of your baby's life, especially as there are so many programmes and DVDs that are made specifically for babies. However, research in the USA ('Early television exposure', Christakis, 2004) suggests that babies under two who were regularly propped up in front of the television were more likely to have poor concentration and there was evidence that these babies could develop attention deficit disorder (ADD) later on.

The French broadcasting authority has banned TV channels from claiming shows are suitable for children under three years old. Foreign channels with programmes for babies will have to broadcast the following message: watching television can slow the development of children under three, even when it involves channels aimed specifically at them. (See 'Taking it further', TV and young children, page 236–7.)

Of course, there are moments in the day when it is very tempting to pop your baby in the bouncing cradle or play nest in front of a programme devised for babies while you prepare a meal or get ready to go shopping but it might be worth considering if a mobile or a toy might be more suitable and just as successful at entertaining her.

'Babies require face-to-face interaction to learn' says Dr Vic Strasburger, professor of paediatrics at the University of New Mexico School of Medicine and a spokesperson for the American Academy of Pediatrics. 'They don't get that interaction from watching TV or videos. In fact, the watching probably interferes with the crucial wiring being laid down in their brains during early development' (*Time*, 2007 – see 'Taking it further', page 236).

Television is not the root of all evil but there is a danger that it distracts you from opportunities to talk to your baby. If you are used to having the television or the radio on all day then realistically this is going to cut down on the quality and quantity of interaction you have with your baby. Babies do sleep (even the most sleep-phobic ones!) and it might be best to restrict your television viewing to those times.

Frequently asked questions

I love chatting to our four-month-old baby daughter but my partner says he feels silly talking when he knows the baby can't understand. Who's right?

Your partner is absolutely right when he says that your baby cannot understand what you are saying to her but you can be sure that when you talk to her she is getting the most important message of all – that she is the centre of your attention. She will be responding to your tone of voice which will be soothing or stimulating depending on circumstances. Your baby needs to hear both your voices in this comforting environment of language. Try to convince your partner that although conversation with young babies starts off rather one-sided, your baby will be eager to respond as soon as she can and together you will be giving her the best possible start for talking and eventually for reading.

My baby is five months old. Is there any point in joining a library or should I wait until he is older?

Five months is not too young for your baby to join the library. There are lots of books suitable for babies. You will discover which books are his favourites (and yours!). Then you might like to buy your own copy. If you're not sure which books are suitable for your young baby, do ask advice from the librarian.

My six-month-old baby falls asleep as soon as I start reading to her. Should I give up even trying to read to her as she obviously doesn't enjoy it?

Don't be so sure she isn't enjoying it! Falling asleep might be the highest accolade she can give you! It shows that she is completely relaxed and that is a lovely situation in which to share books. You could try sharing books with her when she wakes from her nap. Remember book sharing times with young babies need only last three minutes. It's much better to read little and often rather than spend too long at each session.

When I am talking to my seven-month-old baby I talk to him in English but his father uses Polish. Is this going to muddle my baby?

At this early stage the important thing is for your baby to associate the sound of your voices with pleasure and comfort. He can do this just as well in Polish or English. There is plenty of research to suggest that being surrounded by two (or more) languages can only enrich a child's experience.

At my baby's eight-month health check he appears to have some hearing loss. This was not picked up at his newborn hearing screening test. Is there anything different I should do when sharing a book?

If you think your baby might not hear clearly then when you read to him say the words a little slower. Ensure other adults around your baby speak distinctly to him. There is no need to restrict the amount of language you use with your baby. In some ways he needs more exposure to speech so that he can focus his hearing on your voice. When you share rhymes with your baby sit him facing you on your knee, then he can see your face as well as hear your voice. You may find baby signing (see page 31) is a way of increasing the opportunities for communication with your baby. Be sure that you and your partner both learn the signs then, when sharing a book with your baby, either of you could add the relevant sign for the pictures to reinforce the word and its meaning. If you are still concerned seek further medical advice.

Should I introduce lots of new books to my nine-month-old baby or should we look at the same books again and again?

At this early stage you can do both! The excitement of looking at some new pictures will be just as great as the pleasure of re-visiting old favourites. Later on your child may develop particular preferences and then re-reading the same books may be what she needs (and demands!).

I have a four-year-old and a baby of ten months. My four-year-old likes to relax in front of the television when he gets home from school. Is it OK if my baby watches with him?

While it is tempting to have both children quietly sitting in front of the television you need to be aware that your baby is not really getting much stimulus from this experience. He may enjoy seeing his older brother laughing at the programmes but it is not a language-rich environment for him. What about making it a quiet time for yourself and joining them on the sofa? That way you can talk about the television images to your baby in a language he can respond to. Always give your baby a selection of toys to play with (or books to look at) while the television is on so that he does not sit passively looking at something he cannot understand. (For advice on four-year-olds watching television see Chapter 05.)

I talk to my 11-month-old baby a lot. Should I use simple words or just talk naturally?

At this early stage you are primarily surrounding your baby with a wealth of language, and so you do not need to modify all the language you use with your baby. However, at 11 months your baby is beginning to pick out a few important words from your speech. Words like 'dinner', 'bath' and 'sleep' will become familiar to her and you can focus on just a few simple phrases when you are speaking directly to her or wanting her to specifically respond, for example: 'Time for your bath', 'Dinner time. Yum! Yum!', 'Fingers!' (as they crawl near a door).

Summary

- Remember it is never too early to share books with your baby.
- Try to ensure your child is calm and comfortable before you begin sharing a book.
- Talk to your child as you show the pictures or read the words.
- Relax and enjoy your book sharing sessions. Give up if your baby is not in the mood and try again later.
- Try to provide a TV-free zone for your baby.

03

reading and your toddler (1–2 years)

In this chapter you will learn:
- how to develop talk through reading
- how to have fun with rhymes
- how to share books with your toddler
- what kind of books your toddler will enjoy.

*The experiences of childhood create the adult brain.
Between birth and three, children slowly lay the
foundations ... If they can establish strong healthy neural
networks – learning through pleasurable interaction with
loving adults – all their later learning will be built on solid
foundations.*

Sue Palmer, *Detoxing Childhood* (2007)

For children the time between 12 months and 24 months
represents an amazing development in all sorts of ways – from
crawling to running, from being entertained to entertaining
themselves and from babbling to talking. The speed of growth
in all these areas varies from one child to the next. The early
walker may be slower to talk. The chatty baby may be content
to sit and wait for toys to be handed to him rather than setting
off to explore his world by crawling. The opportunities for
parents to support these exciting new skills are endless.

Developing talk

While a baby is still in his mother's womb he is beginning to
learn to recognize the speech patterns of his mother's language.
By the time he is 12 months he begins to link words with
meanings. At 18 months he is beginning to develop a spoken
vocabulary which, by the time he is two years of age, could have
grown to around 200+ different words (this number goes up
considerably when all the 'versions' of a word are added, for
example, drink, drinks, drinking, drank).

How do children acquire this language? Easy! They learn it
from you talking to them. The toddler learns by imitation. If
your baby is fed a constant diet of language he will strive to
copy the sounds you make. You will naturally reward your baby
with extra smiles and cuddles when he makes sounds similar to
the ones you made. This reward will stimulate him to try harder
at those particular sounds and before you know it the
indecipherable babble has become speech that you understand
(although visitors might need a bit of translation!).

Once they start on the language game there is no stopping them!
It is estimated that by their second birthday, children are
hoovering up words at a rate of one every two hours!

Talking to your toddler

Some parents (particularly dads!) might feel silly conducting lengthy conversations with a toddler who might not appear to be listening, never mind replying. Reading aloud to your toddler might make you feel less self-conscious because there are occasions in adult life where reading aloud is not accompanied by spoken response from the audience: think about stories told on the radio or 'talking books' in the car.

Experts in language development say that enjoying 'proto-conversations' with toddlers (treating them as if they can fully understand all we are saying), and truly listening to them, is the best way to promote their language development.

Talk while you push!

Research from the University of Dundee (2008) found that the modern trend of having a child's buggy facing forwards (i.e. away from the pusher) is seriously affecting the amount of parent-child interaction. Children who faced the pusher were more likely to laugh more, sleep more and show less signs of stress than those who were obliged to face the outside world alone.

Talking and understanding

It is estimated that children can understand about five times as many words as they say. So a typical 18-month-old toddler may be able to say about 50 words but he probably understands about 250 words. Because you are only hearing the 50 words, you might imagine that is the limit of his vocabulary but, like an iceberg, there is a lot going on below the surface. If words are to cross over from being understood to being spoken, they need a lot of support and opportunity for practice. Books with their repetition of language and accompanying pictures enable your toddler to link words with meanings.

The bilingual home

Toddlers who are reared in homes where two or more languages are spoken have a great advantage. Their ears are becoming accustomed to the different ways languages are produced. Often a toddler will have a 'preferred' language out of those he hears spoken at home. He will understand more in that language but he quickly learns how the different adults in his life communicate with them and he will respond accordingly. There are a good number of toddler books published in a wide variety of languages (see 'Taking it further, page 235) but you do not need to only use books written in your home language. As you read to your toddler you could simultaneously translate from one language to another. Alternatively parents could make up simple little stories in their own language and repeatedly share these with their toddler. The toddler will then begin to absorb the language of stories in both languages.

Playing with language

Apart from using talk to accompany the things you do with your toddler, you could introduce a rich source of language by sharing little rhymes with him. Most toddlers love action rhymes.

What is an action rhyme?

Action rhymes are little rhymes or songs which have accompanying actions. The simplest of these involves hand actions performed by the adult on their toddler. All toddlers enjoy someone gently tickling them and the action rhyme 'Round and Round the Garden' is the perfect way to do this.

Trace a circle on your child's open palm and say:

> Round and round the garden, like a teddy bear.
> One step, two step
> And tickle you under there.

As you say the last line you gently tickle your toddler under the arm.

Why share action rhymes?

Your toddler quickly recognizes the sequence of this little rhyme from its gentle beginning to its exciting end and most toddlers will be squirming with delight long before you get to the tickling bit! These action rhymes forge a strong link between words and actions and help a child make sense of language and also to anticipate what is coming next. It is also a very enjoyable introduction to the turn-taking principle of communication.

Other popular action rhymes suitable for the young toddler include 'This Little Piggy Went to Market' where you touch each toe in turn until you come to the little toe and as the little piggy runs away home going 'Wee wee wee' the child is tickled all over.

Physically adventurous toddlers love being joggled on a knee and lots of rhymes fit with this action. The rhyme 'This is the Way the Ladies Ride' has the added attraction of a build-up of the speed of joggling and ends with a tumble as you let the toddler (nearly) slip down between your knees.

How do action rhymes pave the way to reading?

If you regularly share action rhymes with your toddler then two things will happen:

1 He will become familiar with the rhyme and its action and will be eager to join in.
2 He will associate the action with the words and make the link between the word and its meaning. All action rhymes have a sequence of actions which he will be able to anticipate. Later on when you begin to share stories with a sequence of events with him he will be familiar with the concept of one thing leading to another and will have the concentration to wait for the next action to occur in expectation of the exciting ending.

The magical world of books

The language your toddler picks up first is the language you use to accompany their everyday activities – 'Let's go to the park.', 'It's dinner time!', 'Look at the plane.' From this 'speech stream' children pick out the key words 'park', 'dinner', 'plane' and these are the words they will try to copy. These early conversations between you and your toddler will, of course, be restricted by what you see and do. However, if we want to explore vocabulary beyond the everyday, then we need to turn to the world of books. Books open up new worlds for everyone and no one is more excited by this than the toddler. The books you share with him do not just need to reflect back his world (although the reassurance of familiar things will always appeal!). Books can introduce to toddlers, as young as 12 months, the concept of a crocodile or a cement mixer or even a talking fox. Reading to your toddler will extend his vocabulary and tune him in to the rich experience of book language.

How long should a book sharing session last?

If, when you produce a book to share, your toddler settles down, nestles into your lap and relaxes, then you can be sure that your toddler is associating books with enjoyment.

If your child is looking at the pictures with interest, then he is demonstrating a positive attitude towards books that you can encourage. However, just because your toddler may only want to focus on a book for one minute, this is nothing to worry about. A toddler's concentration span varies from day to day and from hour to hour. Some days he may look at a book with you for up to ten minutes and on other days one minute might be all he can manage.

Top tip

Don't force your toddler to look at a book if he really isn't in the mood, but keep on tempting him with book sharing sessions – he will come round!

What if your child doesn't seem to like books?

All children go through phases and book sharing is no different from anything else. If he struggles to get away and begins to grizzle, then you can be pretty sure that he does not want to do this activity at that moment. There is no point in trying to insist that he shares a book with you.

However, it does not mean that he would not be interested a bit later or the next day. Keep persevering and soon your baby will associate looking at pictures in a book with a relaxed and comforting time with you.

Lift-the-flap books

If your toddler seems uninterested in just watching and listening then he might like to try something a bit more active. This is where books with simple interaction can be useful. Look for sturdy books with simple fold down flaps. Demonstrate how to lift a flap to find a hidden creature or just hide a picture under your hand and ask him 'Where has the teddy gone?' Allow him to prise away your fingers to reveal the teddy. Some toddlers love this interaction and need this extra activity for their interest in books to be aroused.

How to share books with your toddler

At first your toddler will be happy to just enjoy sitting snuggled up to you as you turn the pages of a book and he hears the repeated patterns of language you use. Then he begins to notice the clear pictures in the book and to follow your finger as you point out the teddy or the fire engine or whatever is featured in the picture. These skills are the foundation of concentration and will lead, in due course, to your baby listening, following and joining in stories as you read to him. If you share the same book many times with your toddler you will notice that he joins in to the tune of the words you are saying. He may not be able to say the actual words but he can remember how the pattern of the language sounded and he will delight in participating. It is through this relaxed and enjoyable interaction with pictures and print that much of a child's future attitude to books is laid down.

> **Top tip**
>
> Regularly sharing books with very young children is a very important way of extending their vocabulary and confirming the association between the sound of a word and a representation of that object in a book.

Don't rush!

It is worth remembering that it is better to read one book quite slowly, enjoying the words and pictures, rather than steaming through a few books very quickly. Your toddler will need some time to focus on the picture in the book and to link it with the words you are saying. Think how frustrating it must be for your toddler if just as he organizes his hand and arm to point at the teddy or the tractor in the book you have turned over to the next page!

Top tip

Some books have busy pictures with lots for you and your toddler to explore. Don't feel you must share every page in the book. A few pages at a time may well be enough.

When to share books with your toddler

Many parents assume that bedtime is the perfect time for sharing a book with their toddler. They are probably hoping that this relaxing time after a bath will be the ideal preparation for a good night's sleep (both for them and their toddler!). Bedtime is a really good time to sit quietly with your toddler and share a book but it's not the only time to share books together. Sometimes toddlers are too sleepy to really enjoy the book. Some parents may prefer to use this time to sing lullabies to their toddler but if you limit your book sharing times with your toddler just to bedtime you are both missing out on so many wonderful book experiences.

You could share books throughout the day:

- to re-introduce your toddler to the world after his morning nap
- to fill a gap at a mid-morning break
- to let your toddler relax after an energetic play in the park
- after a time when either of you has felt a bit fraught!
- when you first get home from work
- to distract him during that fractious time just before tea
- while he eats his tea (and you grab a welcome cuppa).

Top tip

The more times you choose to share books with your toddler the more familiar he will become with the routine and the more pleasure he will gain from books.

A day in the life of a toddler and her books

Sameema is 21 months old. She usually wakes around 6.30 a.m. She is just beginning to remember to roll to the side to look at her cot bumper book. This soft fabric book is fixed to the inside of her cot using Velcro tabs and it folds out in a concertina-style to create separate friezes on each side. Her mum can hear her babbling to herself as she looks at all the familiar pictures.

After the busy changing and breakfast routine and after Sameema's dad has taken her older brother to school, her mum tries to make time for a quiet cuddle with a book before she takes her to the childminder. Her mum finds that using a very familiar book at this time helps Sameema to tune in to the routine that Mummy will be going to work soon.

Sameema's childminder looks after three children under four. She welcomes the children with a drink and a finger of toast and together they share a favourite board book of animals or toys.

Just before the mid-morning nap, the childminder shares a book with each child individually. Sameema likes 'activity' books where she looks for the hidden duck or lifts one of the large sturdy flaps.

In the afternoon, after an outing to the park or shop, the childminder chooses from a selection of action rhymes for all the children to join in with, such as 'The Wheels on the Bus' or 'Row, Row, Row Your Boat'.

After the youngest child has been collected, the childminder takes Sameema and the other child to school to collect Sameema's brother. On the double buggy there are clip-on board books for the toddlers to explore while they wait in the playground. Once they are back home, Sameema's brother watches children's television while the childminder plays with the younger children.

Just before the mums arrive to collect the children the childminder puts on a favourite DVD for all the children to watch. She selects one episode from a DVD such as 'Bob the Builder'™ or 'Postman Pat'® and she encourages Sameema's brother to tell the others what is going on. If there is time, they watch it again.

Once they are home and have had tea, Sameema's mum likes to spend some time hearing her son read his book from school. Sometimes Sameema sits quietly on her mum's lap and listens too, but other times she prefers to play with her toys.

Sameema is never really bothered with plastic bath books but she loves her foam bath toys that stick on the side of the bath. She puts the pictures in a row beside her and talks as she plays with them.

At bedtime Sameema's mum always spends at least ten minutes sharing books with her and settling her down for the night ahead. This is the time for quiet and gentle tales. Sameema gets drowsy as the reading time comes to a close and her mum puts her in her cot.

What books will my toddler enjoy?

As your toddler grows he will be able to sustain interest in a topic of a book for longer. At first, he was delighted with 'naming books' – books which have just one or two pictures per page and where there is no continuity in the action from page to page. In a 'naming book' there might be a picture of a kitten on one page and a mug on the next. Now he is ready to enjoy books in which each page (or two pages) are 'themed'. 'Themed' books are not the same as stories where the events at the beginning build up to some conclusion at the end. In a 'themed' book the toddler is encouraged to see the connections between objects but there is not a single thread of narrative running through the book.

'Themed' books

'Themed' books can include:

• tactile books where the toddler is invited to stroke the soft fur of the puppy on one page and on the next page to feel the puppy's scratchy paws
• books showing a large picture of a kitchen with smaller pictures of kitchen objects in a border around the main picture. (The next page in the book could do the same thing based on the bedroom.) These often develop into 'Can you find the yellow duck?' activities
• a book of colours with four to five objects of the same colour on one page.

Very first story books

As your toddler gets nearer to two years of age he will enjoy following a simple sequence of actions in a book, for example, seeing a kitten playing with a ball of wool and then that same kitten lapping up some milk and then sleeping on a cushion. This is an important stage of development. He is beginning to understand how events link together. Don't be too ambitious about how much 'plot' your toddler can follow. It is best to keep to books which have four or five linked actions and which round off very comfortably and happily, for example, finding the lost teddy, or a walk around a farm to say hello to all the farm animals.

Top tip

Many books now come with the main character as a soft toy. Children love to hold the toy as they hear the words of the story.

Case study: Molly aged 14 months

Molly's mum loves sharing books with her and Molly gives a big smile when she cuddles up with her mum to share a book. When Molly was younger her mum used chunky board books and fabric books which just had one clear, bright picture on each page and Molly learned to look at the picture. Now Molly likes to get in on the act and her mum has found that tactile books (books with different fabrics to feel) are more exciting for Molly. Molly loves reaching out and touching the different textures of the fabrics. She is also beginning to imitate some of the sounds her mum makes in reaction to the touching. She can say 'ahh' as she touches the soft fur of a kitten and make a funny little noise to indicate that something is a bit rough to feel.

What is Molly learning?

- Molly is learning that the times she spends with her mum sharing books are happy times. Indeed she is often the one who starts the book sharing session by pointing at her favourite book or holding it out for her mum to read.
- She is developing concentration and can look purposefully at the pictures as her mum points out things to notice. She is

beginning to understand that the two-dimensional objects in a book are like the three-dimensional objects in her world, for example, a mug or a teddy. She also knows that these are representations and they are not real (although she loves pretending to eat the picture of the banana or to kiss the teddy).

- As her mum talks to her about the pictures – 'Look at the naughty puppy! What is he doing now?' – Molly is learning to respond with a sound. This is the beginnings of conversation and turn-taking and although Molly is not responding with actual words (or very few words), she is demonstrating 'conversation-like' behaviour which will be the foundation for conversation as her capacity to talk develops. She is listening carefully and beginning to copy some of the sounds her mum makes, for example, 'Mmmmmmm' when she sees a picture of a strawberry.

Case study: Jake aged 18 months

Jake's mum says that he gets very enthusiastic when she shares books with him, particularly 'lift-the-flap' or 'pop-up' books and on occasions some pages have got torn so she has decided to store these books on a shelf out of Jake's reach. However, she makes sure that Jake can easily find and play with lots of more durable books. At the moment his favourite books are those with an accompanying toy such as 'Spot the dog' and he loves cuddling the toy as he shares in the story.

Jake's mum reads to him at least twice a day but he is more than happy to browse through his books when playing on his own. His mum has noticed him beginning to make matching sounds as he looks at the pictures – a moo for the cow or a woof for the dog.

His mum has registered him at two local libraries and he loves an outing to choose different books. His mum says that when they get home to read the books, Jake makes it very clear if he likes a book or not and he will push some books out of her hand! She can't work out what it is he likes or dislikes but he certainly knows his own mind. She has decided that the best thing to do is to choose a wide selection and just set aside those that don't take his fancy!

What is Jake learning?

- Jake is learning that some books have special features but that we have to be careful with those books.
- He is learning to incorporate books into all sorts of play situations and he turns to them just as readily as he might choose a toy. He is making books part and parcel of his life.
- He is making associations between certain toys and illustrations of these toys in books and beginning to extend the story life of a character such as Spot or the Gruffalo by playing with them in his toy garage and farm.
- He can remember some of the sounds and words his mum used when looking at the pictures in a book and he can now produce these himself when he sees a picture.
- He is learning that there are lots of books to enjoy and that all readers have favourites which they will want to read again and again.

Case study: Connor aged 21 months

Connor's mum says that for a few weeks now Connor has been fascinated by tiny objects – buttons on his granny's cardigan or a piece of thread on the carpet. This attention to detail is also obvious in his choice of books as his firm favourites are books which have lots of detail on the page and Connor's mum challenges him to find things like the little yellow duck or the green parrot. Connor is getting quicker and quicker at scanning the page to find the missing creatures and his mum says that he seems to remember where they are from previous book sharing sessions.

Connor's mum says he loves looking at toy catalogues and finding pictures of the toys and objects he has. She hopes she is not laying down the foundation for a future shopaholic!

Connor loves to repeat the names of the things that he finds on the page and every day he seems to be able to remember more names than the previous day. He is also beginning to associate emotions with pictures. When he studies a picture of a busy street scene which shows a toddler in a buggy who has dropped his teddy, Connor always says 'Ahhh!' as if to sympathize with the toddler.

What is Connor learning?

- Connor's attention to detail shows his increasing curiosity about the world brought to him through his books. He now has the concentration to study small aspects of a picture and to enjoy the reward of finding something that is 'hidden'. This focus on detail will be a useful stepping stone to the careful observation of print that will be needed as Connor becomes a reader.
- Connor's ability to relate to images on the page indicates a growth in his emotional intelligence as he empathizes with a situation on the page.

Top tip

A great way to get good value books for your toddler is via Internet book sites such as Red House Books (www.redhouse.co.uk), Books for Children (www.bfcbooks direct.co.uk) or even Amazon books (www.amazon.co.uk or www.amazon.com). All these sites have useful offers as well as good ideas of what is suitable for your toddler. But be warned! All publishers like to reach out to as wide an audience as possible and they are inclined to put a very extended recommended age range on the book in order to maximize sales. Ask in your library for suitable authors or recommended titles rather than buy sight unseen. For advice on what books to buy look out for *The Ultimate First Book Guide* (Flynn et al., 2008 – see 'Taking it further' on page 228).

TV and the toddler

Now that your toddler has moved beyond the baby stage, the temptation to use the electronic babysitter can seem irresistible! The opportunity to have a short period of time when you can get on with other things without the 'helping hand' of a toddler can seem like bliss. Your toddler will sit quietly and seemingly absorbed for quite long periods of time in front of the television. But be warned – the experts in child development are worried that too much television watching by the toddler can be detrimental. Research in the USA ('Viewing television before age 3', Christakis, 2004) states, that 'A baby who watched two hours of TV on average per day before the age of two would be 20% more likely to have attention problems at age seven. For a baby who watched three hours per day, this rose to 30% more likely compared to a child who didn't watch any at all.'

Other research suggests that television can delay speech development. It seems that the young child is riveted by the colours and flashing lights, and tunes out the sounds. So does this mean we should ban the box for the under-twos? Probably not, but it is best to be aware of how your toddler is processing the information zooming past his eyes at break-neck speed! Children under two years find it very difficult to follow the fast moving images on the television even in programmes devised for them. Imagine reading the *Beano* to your toddler at an adult reading pace. It doesn't sound a very sensible idea but that is what most programmes are like for the toddler. Television does not develop children's ability to speak because it doesn't talk to children – it talks at them and they can't talk back and talking back is what language learning is all about.

Led by Dr Dimitri Christakis and Frederick Zimmerman, both at the University of Washington, the research team found that with every hour per day spent watching baby DVDs and videos, infants learned six to eight fewer new vocabulary words than babies who never watched the videos. These products had the strongest detrimental effect on babies between the ages of eight and 16 months old, the age at which language skills are starting to form. 'The more videos they watched, the fewer words they knew,' says Christakis. 'These babies scored about 10% lower on language skills than infants who had not watched these videos.' (See 'Taking it further', page 236 for more information.)

Making the most of TV

If you restrict your toddler's viewing to programmes that are specifically devised for his age group and you sit with him and talk about what he is seeing and hearing and you limit viewing times to a maximum of 30 minutes a day, then you can minimize any damaging effects. What you are doing is turning television from a passive activity into one in which your child participates with your encouragement.

What about videos?

The advantage of videos which are specifically created for the very young is that you can play them again and again. In fact your toddler's capacity for replay will test your patience but it is an indication of what he finds comforting and basically he likes what he knows! Watching and re-watching an episode of 'Bob the Builder' with you talking through what you are seeing ('Oh look! Bob has dropped his hammer!') enables your toddler to make sense of the fast moving images on the screen and to relate them to his own experience of dropping toys. He is also gradually able to remember the sequence of actions and so recall the plot line of the story. This is developing his concentration and memory and is the beginning of story comprehension. However, it is worth remembering that sharing favourite books will do all those things with the added benefit that your child has more control over the pace of the activity.

TV and children aged between 8 and 16 months

Some research undertaken by Zimmerman in 2007 (see 'Taking it further', page 236 for full details) found that for children aged between eight and 16 months, DVD viewing of programmes specifically designed for the age group was strongly associated with lower scores on a standard language development test. However, these results were not replicated if the parents watched the DVD with their toddler and talked about the content (which is what the makers of such DVDs recommend).

TV and children aged between 17 and 24 months

The 2006 research also showed that for toddlers aged between 17 and 24 months there were no significant effects, either negative or positive, for any of the forms of media that were viewed. However, daily reading to children and story telling were found to be associated with higher language scores.

So the best way to boost your toddler's potential is to give them plenty of your attention, your time and your language. What we should concentrate on at this early stage is teaching the toddler's brain how to learn through curiosity. Just playing in a sandpit with a water tray will teach a toddler all the following skills:

- fine motor control (filling a bucket with water or sand)
- manual dexterity (passing the bucket from one hand to the other)
- sensitivity to textures (feeling the grains of sand)
- weighing and balancing (deciding how much the bucket will hold before the water spills)

- perseverance (it might take many scoops to fill a bucket)
- problem-solving (how to get the sand from the tray into the bucket).

Everyone wants a smarter child

Naturally every parent wants to give their toddler a head start in life. The world is a competitive place and parents are under a lot of pressure for their toddlers to achieve. They can be persuaded that a certain amount of learning must be acquired before their child is three and invariably the route to this learning is expensive! One of these pressures is to 'enrol' in classes or to buy expensive DVD programmes which claim to maximize their toddler's potential. It is worth saying that there is no conclusive evidence that any of these programmes make a significant difference to a toddler's ability to interact with the world and develop his brain power.

Parents shouldn't feel they have to spend a lot of money giving their children the best start in life. Professor Barry Zuckerman of the Department of Pediatrics at Boston University School of Medicine (2008) argues that the miracle ingredient to stimulate a toddler's brain is nothing more fancy than the book.

'You can imagine if someone technologically came up with a widget that would stimulate all aspects of a two-year-old's development, everyone would want to buy it,' he said in his study. 'That widget would be a book!'

His review of studies shows that children who are read to from an earlier age have better language development and tend to have better language scores later in life. Even getting children to grip pages with their thumb and forefinger will improve their motor skills.

Most importantly Zuckerman found that reading aloud is a period of shared attention and emotion between parent and child which reinforces reading as a pleasurable activity. 'Children ultimately learn to love books because they are sharing it with someone they love,' he said.

Frequently asked questions

I have always left a small soft book in my 17-month-old boy's cot and he used to wake and turn the pages but recently he has been standing in his cot and throwing the book (and every other toy!) at the door. What should I do?

It is very unlikely that your little boy is showing dissatisfaction with the choice of books you have left in his cot! It is much more likely that he has learned that if he makes enough fuss in the morning you will come to him. At least he's not screaming the house down first thing in the morning! Just as the interim time when he would look quietly at a book has passed so will this time of book rejection! The best thing to do is to continue leaving a book (and toys) in his cot as he will eventually learn that playing alone has its own attractions. Don't get cross with him or make him feel bad about throwing books around. He's letting you know in very clear terms that he is ready for his day to begin and you will just have to go along with that!

My 19-month-old daughter has no interest in books despite my many attempts to read to her and show her the pictures. She seems to have a very short attention span. Help!

Don't panic! Children are full of surprises and there is no guarantee that the bookworm at 19 months will be the bookworm at 24 months! Don't give up on tempting her with books as often as you can. Keep the sessions very short and make them interactive. She might like to hold the toy which links with a book or explore a lift-the-flap book (or post the figure through the hole books). Don't let her lack of interest become an issue. Toddlers are quick to pick up on things that press your buttons and she might enjoy the power struggle and there are no winners in such a battle – only losers. Chill out about books and spend the time playing with her and talking through little games with her favourite toys.

At what stage should my son be able to follow a bit of a story? He's 16 months and we tend to just look at books with individual pictures.

You could begin to introduce 'themed' books (see page 47) and if he enjoys them as much as the 'point at the picture' books then you're on your way. However, he might be thoroughly enjoying just looking at individual pictures and so long as you are enveloping the looking with lots of talk which engages him then you are doing everything right.

My son aged 20 months only wants to look at the same limited number of books. Will he gain from this and how do I encourage him to branch out?

Children's capacity for repetition is amazing and it is usually the adult who flags first. If he is enjoying the same books over and over again he is obviously gaining considerable satisfaction from this repetition and it certainly isn't doing him any harm. For your own sanity you could try to bargain with him: one book of your choosing and then one of his favourites. You could try to give an elaborated version of one of his favourites – padding out the text with observations and details. In this way you are introducing him to a wider vocabulary range. You could try sharing a book with him at a different time of the day. This might mean that he is not expecting the usual book to appear and you might be able to trick him into trying something new.

I would like to take my 18-month-old son to a library but now that he is walking he tends to run about rather than sit and choose a book and he is rather noisy.

Libraries are used to lively toddlers and most have children's areas where the usual library rule of speaking in hushed tones is not applied! Many of them have play areas and also specific times for activities for toddlers to enjoy. The more times you go to the library the more familiar your son will become with the routine. He will eventually calm down and enjoy some of the book-based activities (at least for some of the time!).

I have two sons, one aged four-and-a-half and the other aged 22 months. If I read a book to my older boy his brother always tries to pull the book away or annoy his brother. What should I do?

It seems likely that your younger son is trying to get your attention. He may feel quite excluded when you and your older boy enjoy a book together. You could try several things:

- Grab a reading time when your younger boy is having a nap (always assuming that he still has a daytime nap!).
- Perhaps you and your partner (or another willing adult) could have book sharing sessions where you each read with one of the boys. You could take it in turns to read with each boy so they each get a fair share of your attention.
- You could try to involve your younger son while you read with your older boy. Let him have a go at turning a page or

even holding the book. Chances are that he will not find the book as interesting as books you have specially chosen to share with him and he may lose interest and wander off! If he chooses to go, this is quite different from him feeling you want to get rid of him. If you constantly have to correct his behaviour then he is getting a lot of attention (and irritating his older brother in a very satisfactory way!).

My little girl is nearly two. She is a telly addict! She asks to have the television on all the time. If I am out of the room she will turn it on herself and settle to watch anything!

It's going to be tricky but you are going to have to be firm! Just as you would not allow her to help herself to a biscuit whenever she felt like it, so you must ration her TV viewing. Decide on a reasonable amount of viewing time, for example, two 20-minute sessions per day. Talk to her about what you will both watch in those times – perhaps a children's TV programme or a favourite DVD. Stick to your schedule but when the viewing time is over have an activity ready to distract her, for example, suggest you do some cooking or go out to the park or build a stacking tower. She may take some time to get used to this new regime but it is worth persevering. If all else fails – unplug the TV!

Summary

- Talking is a habit! The more you talk to your child the quicker he will learn to talk back to you.
- Simple rhymes introduce children to the sound of words (as well as their meanings) and help them to tune in to the slight differences in words. This is a firm foundation for later reading.
- Action rhymes will help your child associate words and actions and make a link between words and their meanings.
- Make plenty of time every day to enjoy books with your toddler.
- As your toddler progresses towards two years of age introduce books with a simple story line for him to follow.
- Keep TV viewing to a minimum and enjoy it together.

04

reading and your child (2–3 years)

In this chapter you will learn:
- how to extend your toddler's vocabulary through reading
- how to tune your toddler into the speech sounds of language
- how to share books with your toddler
- how to choose books with your toddler.

Children are made readers on the laps of their parents.

Emilie Buchwald

The period between the ages of two and three is not called the 'terrible twos' for nothing! The average two-year-old is a bundle of energy – into everything – and the blissfully peaceful book sharing sessions you used to have with your 18-month-old may seem a distant dream! However, it is vitally important to persevere with book sharing sessions in those moments when your toddler is a little more co-operative. This investment of time will pay dividends as the rising three-year-old who has had a constant diet of books will have a richer source of language and a good knowledge of how stories work with beginnings, middles and endings. These are the building blocks for becoming a reader.

Developing talk

According to the linguist Professor David Crystal (1989), when children reach their second birthday many will have built up a core vocabulary of a couple of hundred words. Typically, they are able to name many objects that are important to them – mummy, daddy, car, spoon, bottle and book. Around this time they begin to string words together often in two-word phrases, for example, 'dropped it', 'me go', 'mummy come'. They manage to make themselves reasonably understood (at least by their parents) and they certainly let you know if you have not understood them! They have a clear sense of language as communication and primarily as a means of getting what they want! One word that comes through loud and clear is the word 'No!'

Some first-born children really launch into language at this stage and some second-born children may rely on their older sibling to interpret their wants and so they may have no urgency to develop spoken language. However, there are no rules about this and all that can be agreed upon is that children acquire an amazing range of vocabulary between the ages of two and three. The toddler at age two who is able to say 'all gone' might well be saying 'I've finished mine' by the age of three!

If an alien were to visit the home of a two-year-old, it might be forgiven for thinking that parents are more concerned with truth than with language. For example, if the child says 'Daddy work' (and he has gone to work) the mother is likely to agree, 'Yes, that's right, Daddy has gone to work.' But if the child says 'Daddy's gone to work' and he hasn't, then the mother might well say 'No, he hasn't.' The alien might assume from this that young humans will grow up telling the truth, but speaking ungrammatically, whereas, you could argue, the opposite happens!

Speaking clearly

Although toddlers make great progress in acquiring vocabulary they may not be able to say the words clearly. This can lead to great frustration on behalf of the toddler who believes they are saying exactly what they want but the parents are left to interpret whether 'ber-ber' means 'beaker' or 'baby' and woe betide the parent who gets it wrong! The best way to correct these 'mispronunciations' is to use the word in context in your reply to your toddler. For example, either: 'Do you want some juice in your beaker?' or 'Can you see the little baby?' It is likely that the context will give you the clue as to what your toddler is trying to say. As children get nearer to age three, most sort out how to say most of the words they need to say.

Top tip

If by the age of three your toddler is unable to clearly pronounce any key words in his environment then it is worth seeking professional advice. It is possible that she might have some mild hearing loss which could account for her lack of speech clarity.

Talking to your toddler

The more you talk with your two-year-old the quicker she will pick up language. Up until now much of your talk with your toddler may have been a one-way conversation, but around the age of two most children really want to engage in a conversation. There are many occasions throughout the week that provide you with the opportunity to use repeated phrases in context. Bit by bit your toddler will become proficient at understanding, repeating and eventually clearly replying. So what starts off as:

Mum   Do you want some yogurt now?
Avik   Yog.
Mum   Strawberry is your favourite isn't it?
Avik   Mmmmmmm.

soon becomes:

Mum	Do you want some yogurt now?
Avik	Avik like yogurt.
Mum	Strawberry is your favourite isn't it?
Avik	Stawbee pease.

Developing conversation

In the early days of talking to your baby you might have asked a question: 'Who's got a dirty nappy?' but you would have to supply the answer yourself! By the age of two your toddler will be keen to respond to your questions. Toddlers can hear the intonation in a question (where the voice goes up at the end) and they learn that this is a sign for them to respond. If you wait expectantly for their reply you will usually be rewarded. In order to become speakers children need to hear a great deal of language but they also need a lot of practice in using language. When your toddler replies you can extend her language by commenting on her answer.

Dad	Are you building a track for your train?
Mary	Yes! I's building a long track.
Dad	If you use the bridge then the cars can go underneath the track.

Perpetual questions!

At age two toddlers latch on to the 'question' words and, in particular, to the word 'why' and many an adult has found themselves on a long and tortuous explanation of something that the toddler actually isn't very interested in and can't understand anyway!

Mum	Let's go to the park.
Lily	Why?
Mum	Because it's a nice day.
Lily	Why?
Mum	Because the sun is shining.
Lily	Why?

Then, before you know it, you find yourself giving a scientific explanation of the relative heat of the sun in summer!

Why does the toddler persist in asking questions? Because she has learned it is an excellent way to get your attention and keep it! Still, she is learning the art of conversation – the request for knowledge and the receipt of an answer – and she is hearing a lot of language (even if she can't follow it!). If the questioning gets too insistent (and you're driving the car through a busy intersection) you may find yourself resorting to the answer 'Well, it just is!' Don't imagine you are doing irreparable damage to your child's curiosity or language development. Learning when to shut up is also an important life skill! The persistent asking of 'Why?' does decline around the age of four when children start to ask questions only when they also want to hear the answer!

The bilingual home

Children in homes where two or more languages are spoken often switch between the languages – sometimes within the same utterance! If they can't think of the word they want to say in one language they will choose the word from their other language.

Children in this situation may appear to be slightly slower than their peers in language development in either of their spoken languages but this slower start is only temporary. Most bilingual children go on to be more proficient in both languages. There is not a finite capacity for the brain to store words, so the more words going in (in any language) will, in due course, be the supply of words the child will go on to use.

Extending vocabulary through reading

It is no surprise that the fury of the two-year-old's tantrums declines in inverse proportion to their ability to communicate their needs through language. The chatty two-year-old is acquiring pragmatic language on a daily basis. This useful language will help both of you cope with everyday needs. However, if we want toddlers to acquire a richer vocabulary then we need to turn to books. In stories and non-fiction texts, toddlers will experience a broad range of words, expressions and patterns of language that are not used in everyday conversation language. This exposure to a rich seam of language will effortlessly extend your toddler's command of language.

The language of control

A study in 1979 found that a third of the utterances mothers used to their children in the second year were attempts to direct their child's behaviour. If we do not share books with toddlers of this age then much of the language they are exposed to is the language of control.

Playing with rhymes

An excellent way to tune your toddler in to the sounds of language is by saying and singing rhymes with her. The particular effect of hearing words that rhyme draws attention to the sound of words (as well as to their meanings). This patterning of sounds helps the toddlers and they are able to remember the words because there is rhyme at the end of the line.

Toddlers under the age of two are drawn into rhymes because of the accompanying actions, for example, jumping up as the scarecrow in 'Dingle-Dangle Scarecrow' but toddlers aged between two and three years are beginning to join in with the words of the rhymes and to remember them. Suitable rhymes for this age group are the simplest of the old nursery rhymes, for example, 'Twinkle, Twinkle Little Star', 'Rain Rain Go Away', 'Incy Wincy Spider' and 'Rock-a-Bye Baby'. These rhymes are short and the rhyming words are clear: 'star' and 'are'; 'sky' and 'high'. There are also 'new' rhymes which will do the job just as effectively. Rhymes such as 'Going to the Zoo' or 'Five Little Monkeys' are available in book form, on CDs and on the web.

> **Top tip**
>
> Encouraging your toddler to learn little rhymes by heart is a good way to train her memory and widen her language skills. Don't try to teach her – she will learn all the more quickly if the rhyme is just repeated playfully without any requirement for her to recall it. If you put pressure on her to learn, it will spoil the fun of the session and not result in any quicker learning.

Case study: Zofia aged two years and nine months

Zofia's parents are Polish and at home Polish and English are spoken. At first Zofia just seemed to like the repeated tunes and words of some favourite rhymes. Then she loved joining in with the actions – clapping her hands when singing 'If You're Happy and You Know It'. More recently Zofia's mother has found that if she stops singing just before the rhyming word at the end of the line, Zofia will supply the missing rhyming word (and be very pleased with herself!).

Top tip

If you feel your knowledge of nursery rhymes is a bit rusty you might appreciate the compilation of rhymes in the book *This Little Puffin* by Elizabeth Matterson (2002). This is not a book to share with your toddler as it has very few illustrations but it is a comprehensive collection of rhymes for every occasion. Alternatively you may like to use some beautifully illustrated large format hardback books of nursery rhymes which are a joy to share with your toddler. It is also an idea to have a CD of nursery rhymes for you all to sing along to in the car. It can make journey times less stressful as well as developing your toddler's memory and language.

When should I share books with my toddler?

The short answer to this question is as often as possible! In reality most two-year-olds have a very busy timetable. They have to fit in time at the childminder, playgroup or nursery, take and collect older siblings to and from school, have a daytime nap, eat their meals, play outdoors, play with friends, and all this has to be fitted in before bath time, night time drink and bed! Some days it can seem as if there's no time for reading. However, building in a routine of regular book sharing will be beneficial to your toddler's language development and her understanding of the world about her.

The reading stamina of the toddler aged over two is considerably more than toddlers under two. This means that the shared reading sessions will need to be extended to accommodate this new perseverance.

Case study: Josh aged two years and three months

Josh is at nursery from 8.00 a.m. until 4.30 p.m. when he is picked up by his gran. The nursery has two formal story telling times with a group of children each day but the staff will often share a book with a couple of children if they show an interest. Josh's mum tries to ensure he has two book sharing sessions a day at home but there are days when he only gets a story at bedtime. Josh likes his mum to read to him when he wakes first thing in the morning and if he wakes early enough his mum has about ten minutes to read to him. (Of course, if he wakes too early she tells him to go back to sleep!)

In the evening, after bath and before bed, his dad is home and likes to take over the story sharing time. After a couple of books, Josh gets very drowsy and his dad puts him to bed.

Case study: Sarah aged two years and ten months

Sarah's mother works mornings only and she collects Sarah from nursery at 12.30 p.m. The nursery staff read a book to the two- and three-year-olds after the morning drink but they have reported that Sarah is often unwilling to sit quietly in these sessions. After lunch at home Sarah has a nap and, when she wakes, her mum usually shares a book with her. She says that Sarah loves the one-to-one attention of the session and would like the book sharing sessions to go on longer than she can really manage!

The bedtime book sharing session is absolutely sacrosanct! Sarah will not allow her mum to get away with anything less than three books! Then she settles happily for the night.

How long should a book sharing session last?

There is no hard and fast rule but generally toddlers can sustain an interest in books for between ten and 15 minutes. Ideally you should aim for two ten-minute sessions of shared reading each day. The bedtime reading slot is relatively easy to fit in but finding another block of time for shared reading can be quite challenging.

> **Top tip**
>
> Your toddler will get most of out your shared reading times if they occur around the same time each day. This helps to build in a routine that your toddler comes to expect and she is able to focus on books and reading even before you begin to turn the pages.

Independent 'reading'

One of the advantages of the increase in your toddler's concentration is that she is quite likely to be very content to look at books on her own. Make sure she has a supply of favourite books at the end of the cot and encourage her to look through her books when she first wakes in the morning. Children who have only just turned two will probably need sturdy board books for independent 'reading' as their little fingers find it difficult to turn paper pages (particularly if the cot bedding gets in the way).

Have a supply of books in the car to keep your toddler occupied. Chances are you will know the text of some of the books off by heart (due to repeated readings!) so you might be able to join in the reading even while you are concentrating on the traffic! You might look out for books on a stretchy wire that you can clip on to the car seat. This does save tears (and dangerous driving) as you try to retrieve a book that has fallen down on to the floor of the car. These books are also ideal to clip on to the buggy.

From two years of age, your toddler will appreciate having a stock of books easily available next to the toy box. In this way she will associate books as a viable alternative to other toys. Indeed, she may begin to introduce characters from her books into her imaginative play.

Top tip

While it is a good idea to surround your toddler with enticing books, it is still advisable to keep precious and more delicate books on a separate shelf out of her reach. It might only be through enthusiasm that a pop-up page is torn, but if a book is spoiled it is a shame and this can easily be avoided by you controlling access to these special books.

Picture comprehension

Is your toddler understanding what you think they are understanding? Jean Piaget, the famous child psychologist, described four stages of cognitive development and related them to a person's ability to understand and assimilate new information. He showed that children's perceptual knowledge develops gradually. Many two-year-olds, when presented with an illustration which only depicts part of a person, may assume that the rest of the person has missing limbs! If the limbs are not actually included in the picture the toddler may think that the person has no legs, no head or only one arm. Similarly, a book which shows a puppy playing on the left-hand page and sleeping on the right-hand page might muddle the toddler into thinking there are two puppies. How will your toddler sort this out? When you talk about the story and the pictures she will come to understand the principles of illustration. You do not need to point this out by actually saying, 'There is only one puppy in this story' but, when you talk about the pictures you can say, 'The puppy likes to play with the ball and now he's tired so he's curled up in his basket for a sleep.'

Language comprehension

When you share books with your toddler there will be words that she does not understand but you do not need to stop to give a detailed definition of the word. It is good for your toddler to hear language that is outside the normal range of spoken vocabulary for a two-year-old. Many adults first came across the word 'soporific' through hearing Beatrix Potter's 'Benjamin Bunny' read to them by an adult. But few, if any, children thought to question the meaning of the word. They just enjoyed hearing the word read to them.

Nursery rhymes are full of language that many adults do not fully understand but it does not spoil the pleasure your toddler will have in the sound of the words. Eventually your toddler will come to an understanding of the meaning of the word through the repetition of multiple readings and the context in which the word occurs.

Will my toddler ever grow out of 'Thomas the Tank Engine'®?

Toddlers seem to have unlimited capacity for hearing the same story over and over again. They will request it long after you have grown tired of it. However, your toddler is seeking the reassurance of familiarity and it is important that this emotional need is met in the books you share. Knowing what comes next in the story gives toddlers a sense of power. They feel superior to the lost teddy because they know that it will be found before bedtime. This is a very comforting feeling for a child. It is through repeated readings of a text that the language of the book becomes language they can use. They will begin to become familiar with phrases which they have heard in books and to incorporate them into their daily conversation. For example, a child might answer her mother's request for help with tidying the toys by saying, 'Not I!' echoing the words of the farmyard animals who refuse to help the Little Red Hen.

What kinds of books should I share with my toddler?

Most two-year-olds can follow a simple story line and so the single object per page book which was their favourite when they were younger is unlikely to hold their attention for very long. Between the ages of two and three the quantity of text and the degree of complexity that a toddler can handle is very variable. Some just two-year-olds can sit rapt with attention with a favourite story book like 'The Gingerbread Man' for long periods of time while others at the same age seem restless after only a few minutes. However, nine months down the line this picture can be radically altered and the fidgety two-year-old can turn out to be a model of concentration.

Case study: Matilda aged two years and 11 months

On a good day Matilda's parents manage to fit in two book sharing sessions (although since the arrival of baby Ruby, time for book sharing has been difficult to squeeze in!). Matilda's mother reports that when Matilda was about two-and-a-half she seemed to lose interest in books which had been her favourites for many months. She used to love books in which she pointed at objects she could name but more recently this has not held her attention. She seemed to want more involvement in the book than simple pointing and naming. Her mum introduced 'lift-the-flap' books in which Matilda also had to find a missing animal on the page. These books had a simple story line which Matilda could follow and she loved the interaction of opening the flap or scanning the page for the animal. She seems particularly engrossed with stories about the everyday life of a two-year-old (going shopping, hanging out the washing, walking the dog). After frequent re-readings, Matilda is able to join in with some of the phrases when her dad reads to her at night.

What is Matilda learning?

Matilda is learning that:

- some books invite the reader to participate and as she becomes more dexterous she has great satisfaction opening flaps and pulling tabs
- stories have a logical route
- books can reflect her own life and can be very similar in some aspects and different in others (for example, Matilda's family do not have a dog)
- when she looks at certain pictures in the book then particular words will be said.

Top tip

It's quite a good idea to plan to share at least two books at each book sharing session – one could be the firm favourite of the moment and another could be something new.

Should I only read stories to my toddler?

Like adult readers, toddlers also have strong preferences in their reading choices. Some love the emotional roller-coaster of a story about a lost toy or a silly clown while others hunger for the information in non-fiction books such as books with photos of big diggers or animals. Toddlers need to have both stories and information books shared with them but not in equal measure. If your toddler has a craze on information books then it is fine to concentrate on those in your book sharing sessions. Her interests will change over time (and you can have a break from cars, cars and more cars!).

Novelty books

There are numerous books on the market which could come under the umbrella description of 'interactive'. These books include lift-the-flap, scratch and sniff, press the sound, pop-up, slip in the character. Most toddlers relish the opportunity to have a specific role to play in the book sharing sessions. However, it is also a good idea to share books which have no fancy features but which will expose your toddler to literary language without any distractions!

Books with an accompanying toy

Some books come with an accompanying soft toy of the main character, for example, Little Rabbit from *Guess How Much I Love You* (2007) by Sam McBratney. Toddlers love to listen to the antics of the character and make the toy join in with the action. The accompanying toy does not need to be soft and many toddlers will cling to Thomas the Tank Engine as they hear his adventures. Although it is a bit ambitious for the newly twos, between the ages of two and three many toddlers will enjoy re-telling the story to the toy.

Books with holes!

Some books are specially designed for curious little fingers! They have cut-out holes on each page for the toddler to explore. Through the hole they can see part of the object on the following page and the excitement of peeping through is very enticing.

Top tip

The children's classic picture book *The Very Hungry Caterpillar* (2002) by Eric Carle comes in a board book version which is ideal for little fingers to explore the holes.

Books in a series

Some books come in a series featuring the same characters. The most popular of these are Thomas the Tank Engine, Fireman Sam™ and Bob the Builder. Just as soap operas are popular with adult viewers, so books in a series appeal to toddlers, who like more of the same. Most books published in a series come with accompanying DVDs. Allowing your toddler to watch one episode of her favourite character can be a nice addition to a book sharing session. But be warned, when toddlers are watching the TV it is the action which captures their attention, not the language of the story, so the opportunities for them to absorb the language are greatly reduced.

Wordless books

It might seem contradictory to suggest sharing wordless books with your toddler when one of the great advantages of sharing books is to immerse children in language but the wordless book gives you the chance to be the author! You can tell the story to the pictures and bring in details that are relevant to your toddler's life. But be careful, if you give an extended version of the story one day when you have time on your hands you will be expected to give an equally elaborate telling another day when you may be pushed for time!

'Can you find?' books

Lots of books suitable for this age challenge the toddler to find an object or an animal on every page. Toddlers love scanning the page to find the hidden creature but they also love finding the hidden creature instantly when they are familiar with the book. You can make a game out of this by pretending that you don't know where to find the duck, teddy or parrot. Toddlers love feeling superior to you as they swiftly point out where it is hiding.

Did you know?

The classic children's book *The Baby's Catalogue* (1982) by Janet and Allan Ahlberg was inspired by observing their own baby daughter entranced by the Mothercare catalogue. Toddlers love looking at pictures of 'things' and catalogues are a wonderful free resource and make ideal 'reading' material in the car as it does not matter if a page gets a little torn.

Top tip

If you pretend to name something in the book incorrectly your toddler will delight in putting you right. This is a very pleasurable way of learning – pointing out someone else's mistakes! Try the following: As you point at the orange say, 'Here is a ... banana.' The pause before you get it wrong gives an emphasis to the wrong word and helps your toddler to hear it. Also, over time, this builds up an expectation that you might get a word wrong which helps your toddler to focus on the picture and what you are saying.

Information books

Some toddlers love the patterns of stories but others revel in the information and photographs in non-fiction books. Both of these kinds of books will enhance your toddler's vocabulary and comprehension so it is best to be guided by her when it comes to choosing books. If she is insisting on a solid diet of one type of book you could always continue to offer the alternative type and eventually even the most persistent toddler will move on to other books.

Information books generally have stunning photographs and toddlers love the fact that the picture seems so real. Sometimes they even try to pick up a particularly appealing image or stroke an endearing kitten.

Case study: Isaac aged two years and four months

Isaac's mother despaired of ever getting Isaac interested in books as he would wriggle to get down as soon as she began telling any story. Then his granny gave him an information book about baby animals and Isaac cannot get enough of it (he even takes it to bed with him!). The attraction for Isaac seems to be that there is a puppy in the book and Isaac's family have recently acquired a similar puppy. After a few readings Isaac can name all the baby animals (including the baby rhino). Now his mum says that he is interested in any information book, although he is still not engaged when offered a story book. She has decided to set aside story books for a few weeks but will re-introduce them when Isaac is a bit older.

What is Isaac learning?

- Isaac knows that there are types of books that he really likes.
- He can make links between information in books and his own life.
- He loves owning books.
- He is learning new information and vocabulary.

Top tip

Watch out! Some information texts have too much information on the page for the toddler. She may love poring over the photos but cannot follow a complicated text. The thing to do is to let your toddler look at the pictures but you could choose just one or two facts on the page to read aloud.

Concepts books

Some books are based around introducing different concepts, such as counting, colour, shapes or opposites. These can be a great way to extend your toddler's understanding but do not let your book sharing sessions turn into lessons! You do not need to actively teach two- to three-year-olds – they are learning all the time and if you try too hard to teach something it will take away the pleasure your toddler has in the book and it also sets them up for failure if they can't remember a number or a colour.

Keep it very relaxed and your toddler will surprise you at how quickly she learns.

Using the library

Libraries are a brilliant resource for you and your toddler and what's more they are free! All libraries have a children's section and many have a specialist children's librarian who will be able to give you advice on books to select for your toddler. Most libraries also have 'toddler time' when the librarians read stories to children and engage in all sorts of literary activities. Borrowing books from the library is a good way to discover which books your toddler likes best. These are the ones you might like to buy so your toddler has her own copy.

> **Top tip**
>
> On a birthday or when they are making a special visit, ask grandparents to buy your toddler one of the library books that has become a favourite.

The sound of language

Between the ages of two and three toddlers begin to become aware of the sounds that are in words and to realize that as well as having meanings words are also are made up of sounds. This tuning in to the speech sounds of our language is the very first step on the road to becoming a reader. The priority at this early stage is to encourage toddlers to play around with the sounds of language. The key to developing understanding about the sounds of language is to help children to listen purposefully. Talk to your toddler about the sounds she can hear – different ring tones, birds singing, cars whizzing by, a squeaky gate, Granny's voice on the phone.

'Sound games' to play

The clapping game

Encourage your child to copy a clapping pattern, for example, you clap twice. Can they clap twice too? You can develop the complexity of this game once your toddler shows she is ready for more.

Can you hear what I hear?

Ask your toddler to listen carefully. What can she hear in the house? (Can she hear the washing machine rumbling or a clock ticking?) What can she hear outside the house? (Can she hear a car horn, an aeroplane overhead or a dog barking?)

Dramatized readings

When you share a story with your toddler, try to use different voices for the different characters. Use a loud booming voice for the giant and a little squeaky voice for a mouse. Listening to the range of intonation helps your toddler to recognize the different pitch and tone of the voice. (See Chapter 01 for good ideas on how to read to your child.)

Secret whispers!

Whisper a secret message in your toddler's ear. Then ask them to whisper a secret back to you. NB The secret need be no more complicated than 'Guess how much I love you!'

Rhymes

Apart from sharing both old and new rhymes with your toddler (see 'Playing with rhymes' on page 63) the rising three-year-old is often fascinated by words that rhyme. Once toddlers cotton on to the sound of rhyming words they enjoy generating rhymes themselves (this is made all the more entertaining if it includes 'rude' words – new, shoe, poo!).

TV and the 2–3-year-old

Now that your toddler is perfectly capable of asking for a favourite programme or video, and switching it on (and in some case, programming the DVD machine!), it becomes increasingly difficult to monitor and control the amount of TV she watches. As mentioned in the previous chapter, your toddler may have a seemingly limitless appetite for anything TV based and it is very tempting to have a 'peaceful' hour while you prepare a meal and they are glued to the TV set. However, in 2007 a researcher from the Child Health Institute in Washington, USA, found that 'while appropriate TV viewing at the right age can be helpful for both parents and children, excessive viewing before three has been shown to be associated with problems of attention control, aggressive behaviour and poor cognitive development' (Zimmerman el al., 2007). Most parents allow their toddlers to watch TV or DVDs because they believe them to be educational and entertaining. Indeed, research showed that 49 per cent of parents believed that educational videos were very important in the intellectual development of their children.

Add to this the fact that toddlers seem to have an insatiable capacity to watch TV and seem to thoroughly enjoy it and before you know it, watching television and DVD forms the single most extended activity of their waking hours. In fact American research (2007) revealed that by the time they are two years old, almost 90 per cent of children are spending two to three hours each day in front of a screen.

Research on TV and the toddler

In 2008, France's High Audiovisual Council cited health experts who said that 'Television viewing hurts the development of children under three years old and poses a certain number of risks, encouraging passivity, slow language acquisition, over-excitedness, troubles with sleep and concentration as well as dependence on screens.'

So should my toddler not watch TV?

One thing all the research agrees on is that if parents spend time watching the children's programmes and DVDs with their child then the benefits are maximized and the disadvantages reduced.

Sit close together with your toddler (as if you were sharing a book together) and encourage the same amount of interaction as you would expect when sharing a book.

When you are watching with your toddler draw attention to what the characters are doing and make comments to emphasize an appropriate reaction to the situation, for example, 'Oh dear! She's sad because she can't find her teddy.'

TV or DVD?

When you share a picture book with your toddler she usually likes to look at each picture for a few minutes. Of course, when she is watching TV the images are zooming past her eyes very swiftly. With a DVD you at least have the opportunity to watch the programme many times so that your toddler becomes familiar with the language and images. Soon she will remember catch-phrases, the sequence of events and eventually will be able to tell you what will happen next. This skill of prediction is very useful for later reading.

DVDs in the car

Many parents are grateful for the 'back-of-seat' DVD players that keep children entertained on long journeys. This is obviously not a time when you could be reading to your toddler (in the interests of road safety!) so playing DVDs targeted for the age range can be very useful. Your toddler's concentration will be affected by all the distractions involved in a car journey so it is best to select familiar and favourite DVDs.

If possible, try to avoid your toddler associating all car journeys with screen watching. On shorter journeys play 'I can see' games or sing along to a favourite nursery rhyme CD. Some toddlers spend a considerable proportion of their day in a car seat (to and from school, to and from nursery, shopping trips, etc.) and this could become an opportunity to develop conversation based on recall – 'What did you make in playgroup? Did you go on the slide?'

How much viewing?

It is sensible to limit the amount of viewing your toddler has to programmes that are targeted to the age range and to a maximum of 40 minutes a day. Ideally this viewing time should be broken up into smaller chunks of, say, 20 minutes.

Top tip

If you restrict viewing time to the same times each day this will reduce the amount of pestering you will get from your toddler. It is much easier to say 'This is not a time we watch TV' if you did not watch TV at that time the day before!

Not the three Rs but the three Ts!

Most people know that the journey to learning involves the three Rs (Reading, (W)Riting and 'Rithmetic!). Not so many people know that the first part of that journey involves the three

Ts (Talking, Telling and Thinking). These skills are what we should focus on with toddlers and if this foundation is securely established then it is much easier to build the three Rs on top.

How can you establish the three Ts? You just need to take time to talk to your toddler about everything and anything. You could talk through your day telling little anecdotes about things that have happened to you. You also need to LISTEN!!! Some parents feel that they cannot get a word in edgeways with their chatty two-and-a-half-year-old but this does not always mean that we listen to them! While some of their chatter will inevitably be ignored it is important that your toddler knows that you do want to hear about things that matter to her. If we demonstrate good listening then toddlers will have a model of how to listen. When we are listening to their chatter, we can encourage them to extend their language by asking 'genuine' questions, that is, questions to which we do not already know the answer! These types of question, such as 'Why did you ...?' or 'Did you like ...?' encourage children to become better tellers and it also develops their critical thinking powers.

Frequently asked questions

My toddler is aged two years and one month and although she used to quite like our book sharing sessions (as long as I kept them very brief) she now flatly refuses to sit with me and look at a book.

Don't worry! Toddlers go through lots of phases and one of them might be not liking books! Don't force her to sit and look at a book when she makes it quite obvious it is not what she wants to do. If she is prepared to sit for a minute or so, try a whole variety of different types of books (one at a time!). She might be drawn in to pop-up books or books with a linked toy. The bedtime read is often the best opportunity to share a book with the 'book averse' toddler as she is likely to be drowsy and will put up less resistance! See if she will look at a book with another adult – a grandparent or a friend's mum. If you visit a friend's house try to let your daughter see that other toddlers enjoy book sharing sessions – she'll soon get the idea.

Should I let my toddler watch TV?

A limited amount of TV/DVD watching for the toddler is probably not going to do any harm. What matters is *what* you choose for your toddler to watch (only TV programmes that are targeted for the age group or a 20-minute session of a suitable longer children's DVD) and aim to watch all programmes with your toddler. In this way you are able to help your toddler to understand what he is viewing and you can also guide his response so that TV watching becomes an activity, not a passive pastime.

I have a five-year-old boy and a little girl of two years and three months. How can I keep my toddler entertained when my son wants to read to me?

Your toddler possibly feels left out when you spend a little time listening to your five-year-old read. This is not surprising as the beginning stages of learning to read are exciting for the child and the parent. It is not reasonable to expect your toddler to entertain herself when you and your son look so engrossed in something that excludes her. Try to involve her – perhaps she could turn the page after your son has read it. Perhaps she could repeat what your son has just read or name things in the picture. Let her have her own book and explain that you will look at her book and then she will look at the book on her own while you listen to your son reading. When there is another adult around perhaps they could bath your daughter while you listen to your son read.

My toddler is aged two years and four months. He insists on borrowing books from the library which are much too difficult for him to follow.

Try to gently persuade him that you have chosen some books that you know he will love and so you won't need his choice! You could even try taking the book from him but 'losing' it before you get to the librarian's desk (chances are, he won't remember that he chose a different book!). If neither of these diversionary tactics work, let him have one choice and if it is unsuitable because there are too many words on the page, then let him look at the pictures while you paraphrase the text.

My toddler is aged two years and five months and she wants nothing but books! I can't interest her in other toys. She only wants me to read to her!

It is possible to have too much of a good thing! Maybe what your toddler really likes is sitting close to you having your undivided attention, whereas playing with her toys might seem quite a solitary occupation. Try to avoid such a contrast between an activity such as reading, where she has your 100 per cent attention, and play activities where she may feel she has 0 per cent! Play with her and her toys. Move the dolls in the house to tell a little story, or the cars arriving at the garage, or the horses at the farm. If you demonstrate imaginative play she will quickly cotton on and come to enjoy her playing times quite as much as her story times.

When reading together my two-and-a-half-year-old gets frustrated if I don't let him open the flaps but his little fingers can't manage them.

It's lovely that your toddler likes to get so involved but it's disappointing if attractive books get spoiled. Look out for the sturdier lift-the-flap books which he might manage and save the others until he has a little more dexterity. Some board books have 'lift-the-flap' features and these can usually be managed by two-and-a-half-year-olds. Avoid 'push-the-tab' features as these require considerable skill in moving the tabs and the tab can 'concertina', meaning it will never fit in its correct place again! As a general piece of advice, keep precious books on a shelf away from curious little fingers.

My partner doesn't like singing rhymes to our daughter who is aged two years and seven months, but this is what she loves before bedtime.

What is it your partner doesn't like? Does he or she feel embarrassed at the quality of their singing? Rest assured – your toddler is not on a panel of Pop Idol! She will love his or her croaky attempts! If your partner really does not want to break into solo singing he or she could put on a CD of singing rhymes and join in! Alternatively, choose story books that have a simple rhyming text – then your partner can relax and read and your toddler can enjoy the sound of the rhymes.

I have a son aged two years and eight months. My mother-in-law has bought us a complete set of 12 DVDs which claim to help your toddler to learn. Should I use them?

It sounds like your toddler has got a lifetime of viewing ahead of him! First of all you need to check that you are happy with the content of the DVDs. If you feel they are suitable for your toddler then you need to ration his viewing very carefully. (See page 75 for advice on toddlers and TV/DVD watching.) You might find favourite snippets on the DVDs which you could watch with your toddler. The chances are that 12 DVDs will cover a wide range of skills and while the first five minutes of a DVD might be appropriate for your toddler the remaining 40 minutes might be too advanced. Be confident to monitor and control everything your toddler watches. Just because it says 'educational' on the box does not mean it is necessarily good for your toddler!

My daughter is aged two years and nine months. She doesn't seem to realize that there are rhyming words at the end of a line. Should I be worried?

Absolutely not! Lots of toddlers at this age might subliminally enjoy rhyme without having any real awareness of how it works. Just enjoy the rhymes for the fun texts they are and don't stop sharing rhymes and rhyming tales with her. In this way she will eventually tune in to the rhyming patterns. Picking out two words that rhyme from the ends of two lines is a very sophisticated skill. Your toddler might be able to provide a missing rhyming word if you read all the words up to the rhyme and then leave a gap for her to chip in with the rhyming word.

My toddler is aged two years and ten months and he is hooked on 'Bob the Builder' books and refuses to listen to anything else. Am I stuck with a diet of this series for ever?

No, not for ever but probably for quite a long time! Always have an alternative on hand to share with your toddler after you have read 'Bob the Builder'. One day he will move on (but, beware, it might be to another mind-numbing series!). His need for a particular book or series of books is very real. He is not just doing it to annoy you! The psychological pleasure he gets from the familiarity of the tale is very comforting and reassuring for him. When you do offer an 'alternative' book choose something that relates to 'Bob the Builder' such as an information book about big machines on a building site. That way the contrast between the 'familiar' and the 'new' is not so great.

NB If your toddler also enjoys 'Bob the Builder' DVDs, do limit his viewing to short sessions and, if at all possible, watch the DVD with him.

My toddler is nearly three. She screams if I don't let her watch a DVD in the car even on the shortest journeys. In the interests of road safety I usually give in. Am I making a big mistake?

Generally speaking, watching suitable DVDs on short journeys is not the end of the world but ... if she uses the tactic of screaming just to get her own way this can have much more serious consequences! Provide her with other toys for the journey which might compensate for the lack of viewing entertainment. Alternatively, play a sing-along CD for you both to join in (assuming your voice can be heard above the screaming!). You might try playing a 'talking book' CD for her to listen to, and she can hold the accompanying book and turn the pages. If she is calm for a moment (while she draws breath) see if you can engage her in a game of 'I spy' looking for dogs or cats.

Summary

- Children's language is developing at a great rate between the ages of two and three years. Encourage this development by talking to them and listening to their endless chatter.
- Reading to your child will widen her vocabulary as well as extend her knowledge about the world.
- There are many different kinds of books that will appeal to your child.
- If your child is watching TV, spend time watching the programmes with her.

05

reading and your child (3–4 years)

In this chapter you will learn:
- why it is vital to read aloud to your child
- how to share books with your child
- how to help your child tune in to the speech sounds of language
- how to choose books for your child.

If children are to become readers for life they must first love stories.

Michael Morpurgo, Children's Laureate 2003–05

Chatterboxes

When their children reach the age of three or four lots of parents begin to regret all the efforts they put in to teaching their toddler to talk because it now seems as though they never stop talking! It can seem like an endless stream of chatter from the moment they wake until they eventually fall asleep at the end of the day. You and your partner may feel you can never get a word in edgeways! Of course, this enthusiasm for language is to be celebrated! The child who chats confidently is extending their vocabulary daily and also learning how our language systems work – with a few glitches along the way!

David Crystal (1989), the leading expert on English language, quotes a conversation between a three-year-old child and his mother who are looking at a book together.

The little boy points at the book and says, 'Mine book.'

His mother, eager to correct the grammar says, 'No. My book.'

The little boy, thinking his mother is appropriating his book, bursts into tears saying, 'It is mine book!'

Although much language acquisition is achieved by children imitating what they have heard adults say, this does not account for all their language. Their little minds are busy applying rules with an impressive logic. For example, they are aware of how we use the past tense to describe actions that have happened. But they will apply rules from one word to another so that many three-year-olds will use the word 'goed' for the past tense of 'go'. They have not heard adults use this but they have worked out a good guess at the past tense of 'go'. Every home will have lots of examples of children making language work for them.

> **Top tip**
>
> Jot down any examples of your child making his own words. You think you will always remember them, but you won't. Once the phase is past, it is easy to forget these delightful expressions. (It also makes an ideal way to embarrass your child on their wedding day!)

Using longer sentences

Not only do children aged three to four have a lot to say, they are also saying it in longer sentences! The toddler just concentrates on the essentials, for example, 'Me go car.' Between the ages of three and four, children develop quite complex sentence patterns, for example, 'We are going in Daddy's car to see Granny.'

As they hardly pause for breath it is quite difficult to fathom out exactly what they are trying to tell you. Chloë was chattering away to her mother when she suddenly stopped and said, 'What word do I want Mummy? It is not in my head!' Her mother had not really been listening and had no idea!

Questions, questions

The torrent of 'why' questions that many two- to three-year-olds employ to gain attention declines between the ages of three and four as children become better able to express themselves. Their questions now become rather more purposeful (and on a good day they even listen to the answer!).

Speaking clearly

Parents, family and friends can often understand what young children are saying because they are familiar with the pronunciation of the child, whereas strangers often have to ask for an interpretation. Between the ages of three to four children's speech becomes much clearer and most can make themselves understood by anyone unless they are trying to say an unusual word out of context.

For example, Paul asked his parents what 'cheddar bull' meant. No one could quite work it out until his older brother said, 'I think he means "incredible".' This kind of difficulty is common and it takes many years for children to pronounce clearly all the words they want to use.

Rates of progress to speech clarity will vary from child to child and most inaccuracies are quickly corrected, but occasionally some speech problems are caused by mild hearing loss or difficulties with speech production. If your family is finding it difficult to understand your child when he uses everyday words like 'dinner' or 'garden' it is worth seeking professional advice. You could make an appointment to see a health visitor or your doctor.

Children who have mild difficulties with hearing or speech are not getting the feedback of correct pronunciation when they say words. Consequently they get into a habit of mispronouncing certain sounds, particularly those formed at the back of the throat such as 'c' and 'g'. They attempt their own version of these sounds and then get into the habit of using those versions. This becomes a 'learned' pattern which might need professional guidance to address.

Do boys talk as much as girls?

Researchers have noted that, on average, girls talk more than boys (some might argue this is a pattern that does not alter in adulthood!). It seems to be the case that if boys are concentrating (and getting good at) other things, such as running, building and climbing, they may have less enthusiasm for sitting still and talking. As a result boys may seem less confident and competent language users. This does not mean that their language development is delayed (they are undoubtedly absorbing the new vocabulary that surrounds them) but they may not feel the need to use it while they acquire other physical skills. On a purely practical note, the child who is constantly on the move will inevitably not be present when some of the chat in the home takes place. Children develop at different rates and it is always a good idea to celebrate the success of what your child can do (climb safely up on a chair and sit down) rather than worry about the fact that he didn't talk about it!

Case study: Amir aged three-and-a-half

Amir is a very contented little boy. He seemed to be physically adept from an early age. He could grasp toys at four months and pass a toy from one hand to the other at nine months. Amir learned to walk very early and was running at 15 months! He loves his climbing frame in the garden and can climb up the scramble net in the park playground quicker than any of his friends. He likes dancing and singing and loves it when his dad plays a CD and he moves to the music. Unlike his seven-year-old sister, Malika, who at his age was a non-stop chatterbox, Amir is really quite quiet. He listens and responds both to his family and other children, but he says very little. Sometimes his speech is not very clear but Malika is quick to 'translate' for him. His mother is slightly worried that Amir's language development is behind that of the other children in the nursery. The staff at the nursery have said they feel that Amir's progress is perfectly normal. They stress that his understanding of language is very good for his age and that the fact that he does not say much is not a cause for concern. In their experience, children who are physically competent do sometimes have a slower take-up of spoken language but when they are ready they often have a spurt of language development usually just in time for the start of school. They have encouraged Amir's parents to continue to talk to him, to read and sing to him and also to relax and enjoy their son's physical prowess.

Extending vocabulary through reading

Most three- to four-year-olds become very good communicators and it becomes easier and easier to understand what they want, but this spoken language often uses quite a restricted vocabulary. It is only through hearing the more diverse language found in books that children acquire a wider range of words and begin to use these in conversation.

A three-year-old might say, 'I must be careful' as he has heard his parents frequently say 'You must be very careful' but it is unlikely that he will use the expression, 'I must be especially careful' unless he has had the 'Charlie and Lola'™ book of that title read to him. When he has heard this expression a few times the word 'especially' enters his vocabulary. It is through hearing words read to them, talking about the story and then using the words in their own speech that children increase both their vocabulary and an understanding of how words are used. This is vital preparation for becoming a reader.

> **Top tip**
>
> Before tucking your child up at night talk to him about what you have done in the day and then talk about what your child has done. Telling him first about your day often makes him more confident to talk about his day. A lovely way to end the day is for you to praise him for something he has done.

When should I share books with my child?

Just as the three-year-old's vocabulary increases, so do his demands to have more books read to him. Children who have got used to having a bedtime story are now unlikely to let an adult get away with 'forgetting' or just providing a quick read.

Bedtime is generally the most regular time for sharing books with children but other times can be just as valuable. If you can find time to share a quick look through a book or to read a favourite story first thing in the morning before the rush of the day starts, this can set the day off on a good note. Equally, after a busy day at nursery or pre-school, children often need a 'recovery' time. Having a drink and sharing a book gives them time to recharge their batteries. It is tempting to put them in front of the TV to watch a children's programme at this time but you might also consider ringing the changes by using this time to share special books together.

> **Top tip**
>
> Always have a book with you for those times when you might have to wait somewhere – for an appointment, a bus, a train or even waiting for a meal to be served. A book is a marvellous way to distract your child from the boredom of waiting.

Case study: Hannah aged three years and four months

Hannah goes to nursery three days a week and has one day with her grandparents. On nursery mornings there is no time to share books before breakfast, although she sometimes wakes a little early and looks at a book by herself before she gets up. Her grandparents collect her every Wednesday before breakfast and she sits with her grandfather while breakfast is being prepared. She loves this time with her grandpa and they often look at the same book each week. She chats more and more about the pictures and often joins in with the text as he reads to her.

Her mother collects her after nursery and settles her down with a book and a drink. At this time her mother tries to introduce new books and poems or ones that Hannah has not heard for some time.

Several times a week Hannah's dad gets back in time to give her a bath and read her a bedtime story. Hannah likes to choose her book and often persuades her dad to read several short stories. She is very fond of stories that reflect her own life, such as stories about going on a scooter or the routines of bedtime. These stories are not just simple retellings that she liked when she was younger but often have a problem that is solved. For example, the story might tell of how a little girl fell off her scooter and had to have a pink plaster put on her knee.

What is Hannah learning?

Hannah is learning that:

- she can enjoy books on her own
- she can share books with different people
- she likes to hear some books many times and join in with the reading
- she associates sharing books with times of quiet and enjoyment with an adult.

How long should a book sharing session last?

There are no hard and fast rules about how long a time you should spend at each book sharing session. In reality it will be a balance between the interest your child shows in the book and the amount of time you can spare. The time spent is likely to vary from day to day depending on what you and your child have been doing.

However, it is unlikely that you will get away with as short a time as five minutes just before they go to bed. Three- to four-year-olds are capable of following a story with some twists and turns and many of the books will take between ten and 15 minutes to read with all the interruptions from a chatty three-year-old.

It is important to give your child time to look intently at the illustrations and to talk about them. On one page in a story about some sheep there is a picture of one of the sheep crying. This page fascinated a little girl called Megan who then tried to imagine why the sheep was crying. Was it because other sheep would not play with it? Perhaps they would not give it some cake? Or was it because they would not let it have a go on the swing? Megan's speculations about the sheep's state of mind were endless and she would often return to the page and add further suggestions, much to her mother's frustration as she wanted to get on with some work and this page alone could last three or four minutes!

General guidelines on book sharing times

A good target to try to achieve is 30 minutes a day. Of course, there will be days when this schedule is impossible to achieve but if you set yourself a high standard you can strive to reach it.

The 30 minutes do not need to be undertaken in one block. It might suit you and your child to have three shorter sessions in the day. For example, five minutes on waking, ten minutes on return from nursery and 15 minutes at bedtime.

Top tip

Remember – any reader can help with book sharing, so ask grandparents, aunties, brothers and sisters, friends and neighbours to share the load!

What kinds of books should I share with my child?

Children between the ages of three and four become much more selective in the books that they like. They may enjoy certain favourites (invariably ones which you never much liked in the first place and which you think will drive you demented if you have to read again!). Then suddenly, that book is no longer flavour of the month and they latch on to a different title.

Boys and girls, even as young as three or four years of age, often have strong preferences along gender lines with some books appealing more to boys than girls and vice versa, with girls preferring fairies and mermaids and boys preferring cars and trains. You may as well 'go with the flow' on this but continue to offer as wide a selection as possible.

At this age children often enjoy stories where things may go wrong for a character – a teddy may get lost or Mum gets locked out – but quickly these problems are resolved and everything turns out all right in the end. This is an important psychological message for children: things may be dark but we come through the dark to security and happiness. This is quite different from children aged three watching scary films such as Walt Disney's 'Sleeping Beauty'. This fairy tale has, of course, a happy ending, but it is a long time in the story between the Wicked Queen setting out to kill Sleeping Beauty and the Prince rescuing her – too long for little children to be in a state of anxiety.

Don't forget the library!

As your child's taste in books widens it is a really good time to join the local library and to keep his interest alive with a constant supply of different books.

> **Top tip**
>
> Talk to other parents and carers about the books their children enjoy. This is a quick way to learn about books your child might like. Just as adults often rely on friends to tell them about a book or author they have enjoyed, so children often have favourite books in common.

Use a variety of books

Books they have had since they were toddlers

Just because children are able to understand longer and more complex books it is not necessary to abandon the easier books they had before. Sometimes getting out an old favourite or inviting your three-year-old to share the book you are showing your baby brings back memories both for you and your child.

Books about real life situations

Young children like to read about things that they have experienced. For example, books about a naughty girl who will not use her potty, or a tale about a lost puppy, or an account of a journey by train can be very popular. Some of these books can be in a series by the same author and if your child likes one of them he might like others. These books are slightly more complex than the more straightforward books you read to your toddler. They might have a simple problem to be solved or describe what happens if a child falls over and has to go to the hospital to have the cut stitched. Seeing in books what might be experienced in life is a fascination that continues into adulthood for many readers.

Story books with animals or toy characters

Children also like to hear about the adventures of their toys. Many toy animal stories are very popular and authors can make these pretend characters do naughty things which would not be acceptable in a more 'realistic' story. For example, some animals might be rude to their friends or run away from their family. This is a good opportunity to discuss their behaviour and to talk about why it is not acceptable.

Traditional tales

These are very popular and many contain repeated refrains that your child will enjoy saying with you. For example, '"Who's been sitting on my chair?" said Father Bear. "Who's been sitting on my chair?" said Mother Bear. "Who's been sitting on my chair and broken it?" said Baby Bear' ('Goldilocks and the Three Bears'). Use different voices for the different characters to make the story come alive for your child. (See Chapter 01 for advice on how to read aloud to your child.)

Some of these books are accompanied by a CD and are very useful to listen to in the car or when you would like a bit of peace and quiet! Encourage your child to turn the pages as he listens to the CD.

Fairy tales

We might imagine that stories such as 'Sleeping Beauty', 'Cinderella' and 'Beauty and the Beast' were created by Walt Disney! In fact, these ancient stories were originally told by adults gathered around the fire on a winter's evening. Therefore, it is not surprising that they contain violence, cruelty, suffering and death! Not necessarily ideal bedtime reading for children aged three or four. These stories have long and complicated plots and although there are written down versions, for children closer to age three than four it might be best to stick to the simpler traditional tales such as 'The Enormous Turnip', 'Goldilocks' and 'The Little Red Hen' which have simpler plots and very repetitive text (and which are considerably less frightening).

Classic stories

Some stories have been around for over a hundred years and have become children's classics. For example, the Beatrix Potter stories such as 'Peter Rabbit'. Some care should be taken over which of these stories are read as not all are suitable for such young children. 'Peter Rabbit', 'The Flopsy Bunnies' and 'Jemima Puddle Duck' are great favourites and have soft toys that can be bought to accompany them, but 'The Story of Samuel Whiskers' (in which two rats capture Tom Kitten and try to turn him into a roly poly pudding) could be the stuff of nightmares for young children although they are very likely to love them when they are older.

Other stories have become what might be described as modern classics (published in the last 40 years) for example, *The Very Hungry Caterpillar* and *The Gruffalo*.

Non-fiction books

Many children like books about real things with real information in them and are mesmerized by the amazing photographs. Although by no means the exclusive domain of boys, generally boys do seem to prefer learning about 'real' things. They will look for ages at books that have photos of enormous machines or unusual animals and they want to learn about them.

It is important for both boys and girls to have fiction and non-fiction offered to them. If possible try to vary the choice but if one type of book is in vogue with your child then go with his choice and then after a couple of reading sessions introduce an alternative.

Books that have accompanying DVDs

More and more books that are suitable for children aged between three and five years come with DVDs that replicate the text but add action to the illustrations. Many of these books with DVDs tie in with a TV series, for example, 'Thomas the Tank Engine' or 'Maisy Mouse'. These sets can be very popular with the age group and can enhance the story for the child. Some children like to have heard the story first and then watch the animated version, while others will watch the DVD and than look at the book. There is no research that suggests that one way is better than another. The good thing about these sets is that the DVD and the book are generally the right length for young children.

Pre-school comics

Some pre-school TV programmes have comics that offer further stories of the characters. These are often very popular with young children who like the familiarity of a character on screen appearing in a comic. However, many of the texts in these comics are disjointed and do not flow as well as the text in picture books written by authors for the age group. In order to make the story comprehensible you might need to embellish the reading to ensure your child follows the plot. One of the appeals of these comics is that they often have stickers or tiny toys and colouring activities which most children love.

Books with repeated refrains

When children join in with a repeated refrain they are not only learning the words but are also making a valuable contribution to the story. They are learning that words need to be said with pace and expression and they are adding to the way the story is told.

Some books have a repeated refrain, such as: 'You can't catch me. I'm the Gingerbread Man' or 'Fee fi fo fum, I smell the blood of an Englishman.' Others build up a pattern from page to page such as the book *We're Going on a Bear Hunt* by Michael Rosen.

Nursery rhyme and poetry books

Children are likely to have picked up many of the popular traditional nursery rhymes from singing them in nursery or playschool or hearing them on a CD at home or in the car. These rhymes have rhyming words usually at the end of each line and it is this pattern which helps the child to remember the words. From the age of three onwards some children begin to recognize that some words have sounds in common and this skill is very important for later reading success (see Chapter 06).

Nursery rhymes are usually sung but children are also able to enjoy and memorize little poems. There are suitable collections of such poems available. They might be about everyday actions, such as brushing your teeth, or clapping hands. Others might be about the different colours or numbers that either count up or down from ten. Some are just simple descriptions about things in nature such as seeds growing or the sand at the beach. In order to learn these by heart your child will need to hear them many times. Encourage your child to join in where possible by leaving off the last rhyming word for your child to say. Then, later, you could leave off alternate lines. Finally your child will come to recognize the words that rhyme and begin to generate others themselves.

Wordless books

Some books tell a story without using words. They rely on the illustrations to convey the meaning. These books are very attractive and encourage children to both interpret illustrations and create their own versions to fit the pictures, for example, giving the child in the illustration their name or the name of a friend. It develops vocabulary as children learn to use words to describe the events pictured on the page. It also helps them to understand the continuity in a story where pictures on one page lead to events on subsequent pages. Many young children enjoy 'reading' these books for themselves. They recall the words the adult used when sharing the book. When they 'pretend' read in this way they are imitating reading behaviours and this is an excellent preparation for when they start to read words on the page.

Case study: Adam aged three years and eight months

Adam has not been particularly keen to spend time sharing books, preferring to be jumping on the trampoline or watching a children's DVD. However, he has just begun to ask for more books to be read to him at bedtime and can now concentrate on a book for 20 minutes. He likes his dad to read to him, especially if he uses different voices to exaggerate the characters. He also likes monsters to be involved so long as they are always vanquished! He has begun to mimic his father's reading, repeating the words of the monster almost as an echo and he certainly enjoys joining in when there are occasions to shout 'BOO!' or 'Help!' in the text.

Adam is fascinated with dinosaurs and will spend a long time looking at the pictures and talking about the size of their teeth, what they eat and how they lived.

His parents have found that books that have an accompanying DVD are very popular with Adam. If they read the story after he has watched the DVD he seems more interested in the book and sometimes he asks for the DVD again and then follows the story by turning the pages of the book at the same time.

Adam also likes looking at a book with his friend, Bruno, and they will sit together and talk about the pictures for a couple of minutes. They are both very keen on pirate books and spend some time talking about the illustrations of the ships and the pirates' weapons.

What has Adam learned?

Adam has learned that:

- books are interesting and enjoyable
- books are about things he is interested in
- some books invite the reader to participate and he can join in with the words and 'read' like his parents
- some books also tell the stories of DVDs he has seen
- he can share and talk about books with others.

Top tip

Ask your local librarian or children's bookshop for the titles of popular books and set up a book swapping club with your friends.

Making your own books

Some of the most popular books with young children are those that you make about them and their family. Select photographs of people that are important in your child's life (and ensure that you include plenty of photos of the child himself!). Slot the photos into a small photo album or paste them into an exercise book. It is not necessary to write a text about each photo but when he is older and can read for himself he will enjoy reading such short sentences as 'This is Mummy holding Tom when he was just four days old', 'This is when we all went to ...', 'This is Granddad with his new car.'

This can become a favourite book to take on holiday and to add to after the holiday. Very quickly your child will learn the text by heart and will continue to pore over the pictures of himself very happily for ages.

Encouraging your child to read alone

If children have had many books read to them around the ages of three to four they may begin to 'pretend' they are reading. This is a wonderful and enjoyable time to watch what they do.

They will often pick up a book that they know and turn it the right way up. They open that book, generally at the beginning, and start to 'read'. Sometimes they have the exact words off by heart but don't quite match the correct page to the text. Other times they retell the book and match the pictures to the event although they are not saying the words as written in the book. It is fascinating to hear them say sentences with intonation and expression.

Children who do this 'pretend' reading are demonstrating that they know lots about books. They know:

• that books are held so that the pictures are the right way up
• that you look at the black print when you are reading
• that there are words on the page which tell you what to say
• that the words make sense.

All this information is vital when they eventually come to learn to read for themselves.

What literacy skills will my child learn at nursery?

The nursery is likely to start the following preparations for reading:

• Children are read to every day. The teachers will introduce the features of books to children – such as page, title, illustrations. They will invite the children to join in with the telling of the story if it contains a repeated refrain and they may ask the children to retell the story after they have heard it some time later in the day or later that week.

- Letter 'sounds' are introduced – sometimes children are asked to bring things that start with that letter sound from home.
- Some of the words that occur most frequently in texts may be displayed on the wall and children's attention will be drawn to these words.
- Your child's name will be on their coat peg and they are encouraged to recognize their own name.

Helping your child to tune in to the sounds of language

As children become more proficient with language and clearer in their speech so they come to understand that words are complete units. They can use words that they know in many different sentences. With less common words, children often confuse where the actual word starts and ends. Many children think that 'Once upon a time' consists of two words 'wonser' and 'ponatime'. It is not until they are much older and need to read this phrase that they see that it consists of four words!

The sounds of the letters

Young children begin to realize that words can start with the same sound or end with the same sound. This is the beginning of understanding how, when we read, we attach sounds to letter shapes and then blend the sounds to read the words. It is very important that children pay attention to sounds in words as early as possible. Being aware that two words rhyme (i.e. have the same end sound) is the first step on the road to phonic awareness.

Not all children cotton on to this skill at the same time. Like all things in childhood, things are learned at different rates by different children. Some three- to four-year-olds seem to absorb recognition of sounds without any encouragement, while others seem to take a long time to recognize rhyme or to identify starting sounds in words.

The important thing at this stage is to encourage children to listen to sounds and begin to enjoy playing with them. Talk to your child about the sounds they can hear all around them and play word games with rhyming words. Make up sentences where all the words start with the same letter, for example, Ben bounces a big ball.

At this stage it is not expected that children will be able to associate a letter sound with a letter shape. What they should be encouraged to do is to listen carefully and reproduce the sounds as clearly as possible.

'Sound games' to play

a) Listening to sounds

Name that sound

Sit quietly with your child and see if you can identify sounds around the house or outside. For example, footsteps, the radio, a person speaking, a chair scraping, the fridge humming, a dog barking, etc. Ask your child if he can tell you what is causing the sound. You might like to make a list of all the different sounds you can hear and write it up for display on the fridge or notice board.

Go for a 'listening walk' and try to identify all the sounds you can hear, for example, bird song, the wheels of the buggy moving, a police siren, a car engine, people talking, a baby crying, someone laughing, wind in the trees, etc.

What am I using to make a sound?

Find a selection of about five everyday things that make a sound, for example, scrunching paper, water shaken in a bottle, tapping a spoon on a surface, rattling keys, squeaky toy, bits of pasta, rice or cereal put into a plastic box, or a wooden spoon tapped onto another wooden spoon. (Once your child gets better at this game you can increase the number of objects.)

Show each item to your child. Talk about the sounds they make and let your child have a go at making the sounds then place the items in a box. Put your hand in the box and make a noise with one of the items without your child seeing what you have in your hand. Can your child identify what is making the noise?

It is also good fun if your child has a go at making the sound for you to guess.

Can you clap like me?

Play clapping games. Start by doing simple claps in a regular pattern (perhaps four straight claps) and encourage your child to copy you. Then increase the difficulty by doing a loud clap followed by a soft clap. As your child becomes more proficient at this, increase the challenges with quick then slow claps, different rhythms, etc.

Hunt the 'thimble'

Hide an object somewhere in the room and tell your child that you will help them to find it. If they are close you will say 'Is it here?' very loudly but if they are far away you will say 'Is it here?' very quietly. Then ask your child to hide the object and ask them to help you find it in the same way. **NB** Children are usually a little older when they can take the lead. At first they are so keen for you to find it that they usually run over to the hiding place!

b) Recognizing rhythm and rhyme

Reading rhyme and poetry books

Many delightful picture books are written in rhyme. Read these to your child and encourage him to help you with the rhyming words. After reading the book through a couple of times, read the first line up to the rhyming word and then continue with the second line up to the rhyming word and ask your child to suggest the rhyming word. Praise your child when he supplies the correct word. In a similar way share simple poems.

Singing songs

The more children learn to sing songs that rhyme the more likely they are to come to understand what you mean when you say that words 'rhyme'. Sing the songs together and when you are sure your child knows most of the words leave off the word that rhymes for your child to supply, for example, 'Twinkle, twinkle little star, How I wonder what you _____.'

> **Top tip**
>
> Singing rhymes with actions usually captures the interest of the most active children, for example, marching to the words and tune of 'The Grand Old Duke of York'. There are some excellent books of action rhymes available and if you just Google 'action rhymes' on www.google.com you'll find plenty to choose from (many with video clips) on the web.

Rhyming snap

Select pairs of rhyming picture cards and show them to your child. Ensure that he can recognize each picture and is using the rhyming word you want. For example, your cards may show a picture of a 'mouse' and a 'house', but if your child thinks the mouse is a rat you will have problems! Only select a small number of rhyming pairs to start with, then, as your child gets more proficient you can increase the number.

Place about five picture cards face up in front of your child. Then shuffle the five remaining 'pairs' and turn one over. Ask your child to show you which picture card rhymes with it. Continue until all the cards have a pair. Then swap roles and ask your child to take a card and see if you can find the matching one together.

This can be increased in difficulty if you add some 'distracter' cards that do not rhyme.

> **Top tip**
>
> Commercial rhyming cards are available but making them yourself is often more attractive to your child. However weak your drawing may seem to you, your child is just as likely to recognize your pictures as he is to recognize the pictures on published cards. Some easy to draw pictures could be: cat/hat; ball/wall; house/mouse; lamp/stamp; boat/coat; book/hook; tree/bee. Alternatively you could make up cards by cutting pictures out of magazines.

Think of a rhyme

Make up little two-line verses and encourage your child to supply the final word. For example, 'We travelled far, in Daddy's ____ (car).', 'This is Pat, she is wearing a ____ (hat).', 'This old man, drove a big ____ (van).', 'This little house, is for a ____ (mouse).'

Odd one out

When you think that your child understands the concept of rhyme, play a game of 'odd one out'. Tell your child three words of which only two rhyme. Can he tell you the two rhyming words? For example: dog/frog/cat; goat/coat/wall. It is easier to start by making the odd word completely different from the two rhyming words, i.e. not starting with the same letter. When your child can tell you the rhyming words you can increase the difficulty by adding a wrong word which has the same initial letter as one of the rhyming words, for example, bat/ ball/hat.

c) Alliteration

Encourage children to listen to the sound at the beginning of a word. A good way to do this is to say words that all begin with the same sound. Children often start by recognizing that some words start with the same sound as the first letter in their own name. Hina was delighted when she suddenly said to her dad, 'I know "happy" is the same as in my name.' So her dad started to make up things that Hina could say, that all started with the sound 'h' – 'Hina has hot hands.'

Playing games that help children to listen for initial letter sounds is very good preparation for later reading success.

Granny went to market

Explain to your child that Granny can only buy things that start with the same sound. Tell your child that Granny can, for example, only buy things that start with an 's' sound.

Granny went to market and she bought sausages. Granny went to market and she bought sausages and strawberries. Granny went to market and she bought sausages, strawberries and socks.

Tongue twisters

Tongue twisters are a fun way to help children to play with language and they enjoy the funny sounds that they make when words start with the same letter. For example:

Freshly fried fresh fish. She sells sea shells on the sea shore. Three free throws.

You can make these up or find many on the web. Don't forget: tongue twisters are meant to be difficult to say, so do not worry if your child gets their tongue in a twist!

d) Recognizing syllables

Helping children to hear that words are broken into syllables is very important for later reading and writing success. It is important to start very simply and to establish that your child can copy your easy clapping rhythms first. (See 'Can you clap like me?' above.)

How many claps must I make?

Once your child can copy simple clapping rhythms try clapping to the syllables in words.

A good way to start is with your child's name and the names of his friends, for example, Jor/dan (2 claps), Al/i/sha (3 claps). Then introduce other words, such as Dad (1 clap), Mummy (2 claps), teddy (2 claps), telephone (3 claps), camera (3 claps).

NB If your child finds this difficult, leave it alone until he is older.

Case study: Alpesh aged nearly four

Alpesh has an older brother and is desperate to copy everything his brother does. His brother is in school and comes back each day with a sound card so Alpesh copies his brother saying the sound on the card. His dad likes to play rhyming games in the car but although Alpesh's brother is quite good at this and does recognize the two words that rhyme, Alpesh seems to say any word that comes into his head!

His mum decided to read short rhyming poems with Alpesh and encourage him to supply the rhyming words. He is getting much better at this but still seems unable to select two rhyming words out of three. His parents have decided to leave the more difficult 'games' until Alpesh is older but to try to read a rhyming poem or book with Alpesh as often as possible.

TV and the 3–4-year-old

Television and computers are very powerful learning tools and children today know much more about the world and the people and animals that live in it, than children did 20 years ago. Many children aged three to four will turn to the TV when they have any spare time. They know how to turn on the TV and also how to find the programmes they like! However, it is important not to allow them to watch too much TV however tempting this may seem. The TV does keep them occupied and quiet and possibly children are learning something, but before long this can become the most important part of a day for them and they will constantly nag the adult to allow them to watch a programme regardless of whether they like it or not. It is easy to think that if the programmes they are watching are targeted at the age range then this must be OK. However, programmes for children are now available throughout the day and it is all too easy for them to be lulled into just watching the images without making any attempt to really understand what is going on. They are learning to allow language to wash over them instead of striving to understand all they hear. This does not bode well for attentive listening when the child gets to school. Even programmes that the programme makers claim are ideal for the age group and which are visually very attractive, may use language that is beyond the comprehension level of the young child.

If you want the TV to be a powerful learning tool then you need to restrict the amount your children watch and to ensure that they are fully absorbed by the programme. The best way to achieve this is to sit and watch together; to talk about what you have seen and to turn off the TV when the programme has finished. Controlling your child's TV viewing will allow more time for activities, such as talking, playing games, reading and book sharing, which will lay down sure foundations for future reading success.

Top tip

If you turn the TV off after a favourite programme be sure to have some alternative activity ready for children to do, for example, to colour in a picture, make a play dough model or help you with the tea. It is not reasonable to expect children to just stop watching TV and then entertain themselves. They will pester for more TV!

Computer games

Today there are more and more educational programmes and computer games available to children of all ages. Like the television, computer games can be powerful tools for learning and used judiciously they will help your child in enjoyable and entertaining ways.

What is my child learning when he plays on the computer?

- He is learning to operate the mouse with one hand and to move the cursor to the correct place on the screen. This requires considerable hand/eye co-ordination.
- Dragging objects around the screen without letting them go also requires concentration and dexterity.
- If your child talks about what he is doing, shows you how he is 'escaping from the clashing rocks of Sinbad the Sailor' and

learns how to manoeuvre the cursor then he is extending his language range.

Word of caution: Too much of one thing is not the best use of time. Children should not spend too much time locked into a screen, and allowing them to do 'just one more' can tip the balance between a good and a poor learning experience. It is important for your child to share computer time with you or your partner. That way you will make the most of the learning opportunities that the computer has to offer.

Frequently asked questions

My three-year-old daughter likes story time but she can never seem to concentrate for the whole book. After a few minutes she picks up another book and asks me to start to read that one. Should I do as she wants or insist on finishing the first one?

The stories you are reading might be just a bit long for her to follow and so she loses the plot and becomes fidgety. Look out for shorter books (or books with fewer words) and see if that helps. You might find that involving your daughter with the book, asking her to turn the pages, find something in the illustration or guess what might happen will keep her on task. If this does not help, speed up your reading by summarizing some of the events but always aim to get to the end of the book. You might also like to try using information books where just reading a few pages can be entirely appropriate.

My son insists on looking at every page for a long time. He pores over illustrations and reading time can take ages! How can I speed him up?

Most parents are very bad at letting their children have enough time to look at the pictures – so give yourself a pat on the back because children who study illustrations and talk about them are learning to look intently at details which is a pre-reading skill. However, if you really need to speed things up why not use a kitchen timer and explain that when the timer pings (say after ten to 15 minutes) you will have to stop sharing the book together but he can continue looking on his own and you can both look at it again next time.

Our child is obsessed with information books about dinosaurs. He asks for the same books again and again. I do offer other books and he chooses different ones from the library but still insists he has a dinosaur book every time we sit down to share a book.

Perhaps you could suggest that his dad reads the dinosaur books but that you want to look at a library book on a different topic. Keep tempting your son with exciting books on other topics. Make the book sound appealing by expressing your own interest in the subject, for example, 'This book looks so exciting – it's all about the really big machines that dig the earth.' If this does not work, don't despair – it is certain that your son will grow out of his obsession with dinosaurs in time! You could try introducing stories about dinosaurs or even dinosaur poems! You might even look at pop-up books or lift-the-flap books to maintain his interest.

The nursery that my daughter attends told us that she will not sit down and listen to a book when they read. She gets up and wanders around, sometimes distracting other children who are listening. What should I do?

If your child is happy to sit with you while you share a story with her then it is important that you ask your child why she doesn't like to sit down with the other children at story time. If she does not seem able to explain, then talk to the nursery staff and describe how she behaves at home. Ask them if they have any ideas that would explain her behaviour and ask them what you could do that might help. It could be something as simple as the fact that she loves the quiet intimacy of book sharing at home and finds the public reading not nearly as satisfying. She will be used to your devoted one-to-one attention and may feel frustrated by the different experience of reading in the nursery. If this is the case, she will learn gently that reading at home and reading in the nursery are not going to be quite the same experience. You might ask the nursery teacher if your daughter could sit close to the adult who is reading or perhaps another adult could sit close to her.

Of course, the problem might be something as simple as not being able to sit next to her friends or that she can't see the pictures or that she wants to sit at the front. Some girls, especially if they are rather shy, don't tell the teachers or helpers why they are bothered but take themselves off to get away from the situation.

Our daughter watches TV all the time. She sometimes gets up early and sneaks downstairs and switches on the TV before we get up. She gets quite hysterical if she does not get a favourite DVD when she gets home from the nursery school. What can we do?

Research has shown that children who watch too much TV or spend too long on the computer are at an educational disadvantage. It is not a good thing for children to rely on one form of entertainment and watching so much TV is certainly not good for her physical or mental development. In order to stop her watching without your knowledge it may be necessary to turn off the TV at the mains or unplug it when you go to bed so that she cannot turn it on by herself.

It is also important to realize that if she always gets her own way at this early age then she is likely to be even more difficult as she gets older. If possible, offer her other attractions that will take her away from the TV and DVDs. Perhaps you could invite one of her friends back to play, on the understanding that there will be no TV while her friend is there. You might try to ensure that she does not get straight back home after nursery but helps you with the shopping, or perhaps you could visit the park, etc. When you do get home explain that she can have the TV on for the duration of one programme and then it will be switched off. If this triggers a crying fit, remove her from the TV and turn it off so that she cannot switch it back on. It takes a long time to re-establish behaviours but the longer you leave it the longer it takes to get right. Remember, you are taking something away from your daughter that she really enjoys so you will have to be prepared to put in the time and effort to compensate her for this. She will need your time and interest if you are to find alternatives to compulsive TV watching. Try distracting her by playing or reading with her so, from her point of view, there are enjoyable alternatives to television watching.

My friends' children all seem to be able to recognize rhyming words but when I ask my son to supply a rhyming word he seems to have no idea what I'm after and just says any word that comes into his head or refuses to speak. What should I do?

Don't let this worry you. Some children do seem to be able to understand what we mean when we talk about rhyme but many young children do not grasp this idea until they are over five years of age. As children become more proficient at talking they concentrate on making themselves understood by others. Playing with rhyming words is often closer to nonsense language and your son might be puzzled by this change in the focus of language. When you ask him to supply a rhyming word he might, quite legitimately, be thinking – 'Why?'

Recognizing rhyme is a useful introduction to hearing the sounds of spoken language and will be something that is taught in schools, but it is not essential that your child masters this skill before school. If you think some of the games suggested on pages 100–1 would help you could try these but there are far more important skills than recognizing rhyme, such as developing spoken language and enjoying books together. Enjoy what your son can do and don't worry about things he can't manage yet.

I am a single mum and I have three children under six. By the time I have heard my eldest child read to me and then bathed the 18-month-old there never seems enough time to read to my three-year-old. What can I do?

It can be difficult to set aside time to read to one child under six every day so having three is very difficult to achieve. You could look at how each day pans out. You do not necessarily need to hear your eldest child read to you every day, indeed it is equally important that you read books to him, so you might like to work out which three days out of the seven you could read to all your children and set aside three days when you will hear your child read to you. It is very likely that your three-year-old and the six-year-old will enjoy many of the same books and you could invite your six-year-old to help you to read some of the words. Your toddler will just enjoy being with the others on the sofa! If the school has insisted that you try to hear your eldest child read every day then see if it is possible for your eldest child to read to the three-year-old while you bath the toddler. Another way to let your children hear books read to them is to borrow 'spoken word' stories from the library. Both your older children will enjoy listening to these together and if they come with a book as well, then your eldest child can follow the print as he hears the book being read.

It is really important that you do not feel guilty and pass this worry on to your children. No one can do everything they would like to do with their children, so missing hearing them read or reading to them is not as important as enjoying something all together.

Summary

- Children's language is developing at a great rate between the ages of three and four years. Encourage this development by talking to them and listening to the endless chatter!
- Reading to your child will widen his vocabulary as well as extend his knowledge about the world.
- Provide a wide variety of books – rhymes, stories, pop-up books, books with DVDs and information books.
- Try to limit TV watching to times when you can watch together.

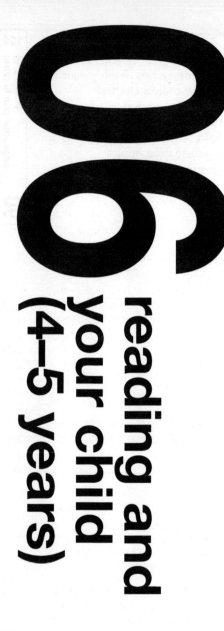

06

reading and your child (4–5 years)

In this chapter you will learn:
- about the language development of children aged 4–5 years
- why it is vital to read to your child
- how to share books with your child
- how to encourage listening to sounds in words
- how to help your child to start to recognize words.

We need to help small children to communicate hopes, fears and joys ... we do this when we share stories with them.

Dorothy Butler, *Babies Need Books* (1982)

Language development

Between the ages of three and five children's vocabulary increases at an amazing rate. Children can acquire as many as 20 new words a day! Adults trying to learn a new foreign language find it difficult to learn 20 new words a month! By the age of five most children have a spoken vocabulary of around 1,500 words (this includes counting the various forms of a word: walk, walked, walking, walks). Those same children are likely to *understand* 5,000 words! Most of their words are clearly pronounced and adults and other children can understand what they are saying. However, a few letters and letter combinations such as 'r' and 'w', 'tr' and 'ch' or 'f' and 'th' can still cause problems. One little girl came home from school and said that the class were making a collection of things beginning with 'w'.

'What are you going to take?' asked her mother. 'My wabbit [rabbit] and my woller blades [roller blades],' she happily replied!

This slight problem with pronunciation is very common and rarely suggests any serious speech difficulty and it invariably disappears over time.

Grammatical 'errors'

By the age of five, most children have mastered many of the forms of the past tense of verbs although some errors may persist (particularly with irregular verbs). For example, children around the age of four may still use 'He wented' but generally by five years they will have learned to say, 'He went.'

When the majority of words are used correctly, any remaining 'errors' tend to stand out more and it can be very tempting to always correct them. Sometimes over-correction can get in the way of communication.

Child Toby bringed a book to school today.
Mother No. Say, 'Toby brought a book to school today.'

Child	But Toby did bringed a book.
Mother	No, Toby brought a book.
Child	Yes, He bringed his book.

The best way to deal with these errors is not to draw too much attention to them but to correct them by modelling the correct form of the word and continuing with the conversation. It would have sorted the problem much more quickly if the mother had said:

'Oh! So Toby brought a book to school. Did the teacher read it to you all?'

This would have maintained a conversation and her child would quickly pick up the correct 'brought' in context.

Speech problems

If you feel that your child's speech is noticeably less clear than that of her peers, speak to the class teacher and see if they feel the same. If there are concerns then do not hesitate to seek professional advice. The school may be able to arrange for a speech therapist to assess your child or you could ask your doctor for a referral. The earlier the problem is addressed the easier it is to sort out.

Story telling

Between the ages of four and five, as their competence with spoken language grows, many children begin to retell events that have happened in their own lives such as telling a grandparent on the phone about a missing car key. These stories are often quite logical and generally have a beginning, middle and end, although sometimes they can be a bit rambling and unless you already know the circumstances it can be quite difficult to make sense of the account! Telling things in a logical order and maintaining the interest of your audience is a very advanced skill that takes years to refine, but helping children by asking questions to clarify the events is the way to start them on this journey.

| Dad | So Mum closed the door and left the key inside? How did you get back into the house? |
| Child | Mum went to see Mrs Jones and Mrs Jones had a key that was the same as our key and then Mum had the key and we got back in. |

| *Dad* | It was lucky Mrs Jones had a key. |
| *Child* | Yes, Mrs Jones had a key and we got back in and then I had drink of milk. |

When children start school many parents worry about practical issues:

- Will my child manage in the school toilet?
- Will they make friends in the playground?
- Will they do as they are told?
- Will they be happy?
- Will they eat their school meal?
- Will they like their teacher?

In reality the vast majority of children make a very smooth transition from home/nursery to school and quickly settle in to school routines. Children who seem to find the transition easiest are those who come from homes where they have been talked to, listened to and who have been read to regularly.

Reading aloud to your child

Children who have been read to from the age of 12 months to five years are likely to have heard in the region of 600 different stories before they get to school. If a teacher read a story to the class every school day it would take around five years before she would have read 600 stories! Regularly reading aloud to your child gives her the best preparation for learning to read. Children who have been read to will have met hundreds of words that are rarely used in conversations but are common within stories and they will also have come across a much wider range of people and things through the pages of books.

They will have laughed at the antics of other children and animals in favourite stories and been momentarily scared of a nasty witch. These vicarious experiences will have given them greater insight into all the emotions that humankind experiences. When we meet characters in books we are told what they look like, what they are thinking, what happens to them and how they feel. In turn we learn to tell stories using the language of stories. We describe how we were feeling, looking and thinking, and present this to our listeners in a logical and interesting way. So familiarity with the language in books not only prepares children for becoming readers, it also gives children a spoken vocabulary which is rich and varied.

The benefits of reading to your child

Research undertaken by M. Senechal and J. LeFevre (Carleton University, 2002) looked at what parents could do with their pre-school children that would help them to learn to read when they got to school. They found three major ways in which parents and carers made a significant difference:

- Parents who read stories to their children developed their child's oral language skills (vocabulary and listening skills). This had a direct effect upon their child's attitude to reading, created a desire to learn to read and resulted in later fluent reading attained by their child.
- Parents who also encouraged the development of word skills (knowing letters, sounding out and blending sounds in simple words) contributed to their child's later reading success.
- The relationship between reading story books and early reading achievement indicated that it is important for parents to continue to read to their child during and after the time she is learning to read.

Based on their findings they suggested that early and continued parental involvement in children's literacy development is very important.

How much time should I spend reading to my child?

Parents of young children live very busy lives and finding time to set aside for reading to their children can be difficult. Ideally parents of children aged between four and five should aim at reading to them for a minimum of half an hour a day.

The usual time for sharing books together is just before the child's bedtime as this is often a quiet time and listening to a story settles them down for the night. However, the most important thing is to have a regular time each day so that the child associates the time with books as relaxing and pleasurable. Some parents find that a good way to deal with the inevitable fractiousness when a child first gets back from nursery or pre-school is to have a quiet 15 minutes with a drink and some favourite books. Some parents even manage to set time aside before they dress in the morning!

Top tip

It is not necessary to read to your child for half an hour at one time. It may be easier to break this up into shorter time spans. It might even be possible to spend longer than 30 minutes reading during a day!

What kinds of books should I read to my child?

As children's vocabulary develops, so too does their understanding. Between the ages of four and five, children's concentration and understanding makes leaps and bounds. They will still enjoy many of the books they had when they were younger, for example, books with little text but loads of things to look at and talk about, but at this age they also enjoy complete stories with characters, action and a happy ending. Both kinds of books are very valuable and just because they can cope with more words on a page it does not mean that we should always read more difficult books to children of this age.

Non-fiction

It is just as important to read non-fiction to children as it is to read fiction. Try to find books that are about things they are interested in, activities that they do or places they have visited.

Although there are plenty of boys who love stories (just as there are plenty of men who love fiction), between the ages of four and five some boys begin to show a preference for non-fiction. Boys can be mesmerized by pictures and facts about, for example, huge machines or about tractors or cars. It is important to allow your son the opportunity to pursue his interest in information books. It does not mean that you need to abandon reading stories to him; it's just a case of finding a balance that suits you both.

Who chooses?

As in so many other spheres of their lives, children aged four and five are quite good at letting you know what they like and dislike! This can result in you and your child having very different opinions about what would be fun to read as a bedtime story. Some children get hooked on books that never appealed to you in the first place and then they want to hear them re-read endlessly. Sometimes it can be difficult to work out why a certain book has become a firm favourite with your child but the best strategy is to continue to read it to her but to always read something else as well and to hope that, in due course, your child's enthusiasm for the book wanes and you can move on to enjoy books that you both like.

> **Top tip**
>
> Some desperate parents, feeling they will go demented if required to read a particular book yet again for the hundredth time, have resorted to hiding the book and then pretending they have no idea where it could be!

Books to share with your child

Select from the following range of books to give your child the widest book experience.

Favourite books from when they were younger

Apart from the fact that hearing a familiar story is very comforting and reassuring, we must never forget that as a child grows, their understanding of a story changes and unlike the clothes they seem to grow out of so quickly, books grow with children. This means that a child has a changing perspective on a story and will see it with new eyes as their understanding about life around them becomes more sophisticated.

Books about situations they have met or will meet

These sorts of books help you to prepare your child for momentous occasions in her life – like going to school or having a baby brother or sister. Your child will see and hear how the children in the book cope with situations and this gives your child an insight into how things might be for her.

Adventure stories

Between the ages of four and five a child's horizon is widening all the time. They become much more aware of things beyond the confines of the home setting and outings to familiar places like the shops, nursery, or the childminders. At this age children begin to enjoy books that go beyond the familiar and take them into the world of imagination – to outer space or a deep dark forest.

Traditional tales

Traditional tales have been told to children for centuries. Children aged four to five have a strong sense of right and wrong and they love the mixture of danger and fear in traditional tales as well as their guaranteed happy ending for the good and punishment for the wrong-doers! Some of the tales are rather long for four- to five-year-olds and for these children the simpler, cumulative tales such as 'The Enormous Turnip', 'The Big Pancake' and 'The Little Red Hen' have plenty of repetition and cautionary advice (help one another, share with others) and greatly appeal to young children.

Books with machines as the characters

Some children, boys in particular, can get 'hooked' on books with vehicles such as trains or helicopters as the main character. The characters in these stories display the whole range of human behaviours and emotions (disobeying orders, being grumpy, saving the day, etc.) that children like to hear about, but with the added bonus that they run on wheels! It is hard to explain the enthusiasm some children have for such series as 'Thomas the Tank Engine' but its popularity is indisputable! This undoubtedly has something to do with the product links of toys, pyjamas and quilt covers as well as the numerous DVDs. It can sometimes seem that these are the only books that children want and they request them all the time, but it is advisable to offer a wider diet of books to ensure your child meets different authors, illustrators and themes. Try to strike a balance so that you read one 'different' book every time you read a 'Thomas' book. That way your child gets the story she wants and you get the chance to widen her literary horizons.

Classic stories

Some would argue that there is a canon of children's literature that should be every child's inheritance. These could be described as 'modern classics', and the authors and titles on the list might vary from house to house but there are some books that have been 'treasures' for children for over a quarter of a century and most parents would like their child to share in this literary tradition. The following list is not exhaustive but it could be the basis of any child's personal library:

The Cat in the Hat by Dr Seuss
Where's Spot? by Eric Hill
Kipper by Mick Inkpen
Each Peach Pear Plum by Janet and Alan Ahlberg

We're Going on a Bear Hunt by Michael Rosen
Dear Zoo by Rod Campbell
Meg and Mog by Helen Nicoll
The Very Hungry Caterpillar by Eric Carle
Rosie's Walk by Pat Hutchins
Dogger by Shirley Hughes
Can't You Sleep, Little Bear? by Martin Waddell
A Snowy Day by Nick Butterworth
Mr. Gumpy's Outing by John Burningham
The Lighthouse Keeper's Lunch by Ronda and David Armitage
What Do People Do All Day? By Richard Scarry

Wordless books

One slightly different way to share a book with your child is to choose a book that has no words. This puts you and your child in the hot seat to tell the story from the pictures. It encourages your child to engage as you tell the events and the book sharing session becomes a voyage of discovery. For example, you might look at one of the pictures and provide a commentary: 'Look here! The mum is hoping to have five more minutes before she has to get up. Do you think the little girl will let her rest in peace? I don't think so! Look – she's trying to sneak under the covers. Do you think the mum will know that she's there?'

Children's comics/magazines

At around this age children love you to buy them a magazine. This may be part of pester power at the supermarket checkout but some children do get hours of fun turning the pages of magazines and comics specifically targeting the four to five age range. The magazines are in a larger format than a book (and they often come with a tempting free gift!) and this, combined with the link to a character children have met on TV or on DVD, may contribute to their popularity.

While these magazines can be fun, it is advisable to read them to your child alongside a wide range of other quality literature. The language in the magazines may be fairly limited and sometimes the plot lines are pretty scrappy (not surprising when one considers the writing time allocated to the authors for the submission deadline). They certainly won't do any harm but as your time to read to your child is very precious it is best to fill it with the very best that authors and illustrators have to offer.

Dual language books

Children from homes where there is more than one language spoken will enjoy the rich diversity of language gleaned from books in both their home languages. Some of these books have a dual text – that is the story or information is told first in one language and then, underneath that, in a second language. Other books may be printed entirely in a language other than English. Children who hear two (or more) languages spoken should certainly hear those languages read to them. There are a small number of specialist publishers who produce these books. Some of the titles are those on the list of modern classics and others draw from the rich literary culture of the other home language.

(For details on finding children's books in languages other than English see 'Taking it further', page 235.)

Pop-up books

Once children are approaching five years of age their little hands are much more dextrous and they are able to handle the tabs, pulls and flaps of these special books with care. It is a particular pleasure to a child if you 'pretend' that you don't know what is behind the flap (despite numerous prior readings!). They love the sense of superiority as they tell you confidently who is there and what is being said. Then they can lift the flap and be proved right.

Home-made books

While there are so many wonderful published books to share with your child, don't forget that a simple book you have made might prove to be the number one favourite! An easy way to make a book is to take a series of photographs to follow a particular sequence of events, for example, a holiday or even a trip to see Grandma. Put the photos in an A5 slip in a photograph wallet and add a simple text. For example, under the first picture of your child waking in the morning you could write, 'On Saturday we got up early. We were going to go to see Grandma.' Continue with a short caption describing the events in sequence ending with something along the lines of, 'We had a lovely day and we will go to see Grandma again very soon.'

If you and your child do not live close enough to see grandparents regularly you might like to ask them to make a 'photograph book' for your child. They need only 'snap' themselves doing everyday things – Grandma doing some gardening, Grandpa having a snooze. Then they could add a simple written text describing the events. They can be assured that it will be a possession treasured by their grandchild.

If you have photos of yourself when young, this can be a source of great fascination to your child. Put the photos in time order into an A5 slip-in folder and add a simple caption such as 'This is me when I was two. I don't look very happy. I wanted to play in the sandpit but it was time to go home.'

Don't forget the library

The librarian in your local library will be happy to help with advice on what to read. They have a wealth of knowledge about books which appeal to boys and girls and which are appropriate for the age group. Don't forget that choosing a book is part of the excitement and at four to five your child will be beginning to have clear preferences. Out of your allocation of six books you might like to choose three and allow your child to choose the other three.

Many libraries are very understanding about the busy lives parents lead and they do not charge a fine on children's books if you have the book longer than the suggested return date. Some even provide stickers for every book your child borrows – a great incentive to young children!

Top tip

When you take your child to play with a friend's children, share good ideas of books you have found popular with your own children. This is an easy way to pick up good recommendations. You might also like to do some book swapping.

Introducing book features as you read

When you read with your child try to introduce her to 'book features'. Talk about the term '*title*' and point out that the title is on the *cover* of the book and sometimes on the *spine* as well. Ask your child to find the *page* where you should start reading.

Invite your child to hold the book and to turn over the next page. Learning to turn the pages of a book requires considerable manual dexterity and children will only acquire this skill through frequent practice.

Ask your child to find something in the pictures and talk about the *illustrations*. Then ask her if she would like you to start reading. Point to the *words* and say that you will start reading from here. Sometimes she wants to turn a page before you have read all the text. Explain that you have not finished reading all the *words* and point again when you have got to the end.

When you talk about the book ask her what happened at the *beginning* of the story and what happened at the *end* of the story.

You do not need to be too formal about introducing this vocabulary but if you use these terms quite naturally children quickly come to both understand them and use them when they are sharing a book.

Top tip

Left-handed children can find it particularly difficult to turn the pages accurately if they are seated on your left. They have to reach across their own bodies (and yours!) to get to the top right-hand corner. If you let them sit on your right then their left hand is closest to the page for turning.

Using TV wisely

As children get more independent and more aware of the world around them so they also ask to spend more and more time watching the TV or playing computer games. It becomes increasingly difficult to deny their requests, especially if you have older or younger children in the home. However, all the research emphasizes the advantages of restricting television viewing to programmes which you feel will really benefit your child (see 'Taking it further', page 236, for references to examples of this research). This early discipline will lay down a firm foundation so that as children get older they become discriminating viewers for themselves.

Television can help your child to learn but if the TV is permanently on then she learns to pay little attention to the content of the programme. This encourages her to treat it as background noise and she will happily leave on a programme she has no interest in. Parents may think that because there is a lot of talking in TV programmes this will extend their child's vocabulary. But the talking on TV is language spoken **at** the children not **to** them. This does not give the exposure to language that children need. In order for children to acquire new words they need to hear them many times in meaningful contexts and to be encouraged to use them themselves. Television cannot provide this exchange of language.

Television teaches children to expect instant gratification but children learn far quicker by other means. A TV programme might teach a child to count to ten but counting ten steps with your child, playing games where you take turns to say the next number, and singing counting songs, etc. are far quicker routes to your child knowing her numbers.

Aim to:

- keep TV or computer time to under one hour a day
- help your child to select the programme to watch or game to play
- watch the programme with your child
- talk about the programme you have seen, the bits you thought were the funniest, scariest, most exciting
- offer alternative activities and remember to have something for your child to do after watching a programme
- always turn the TV off during meals
- avoid using the TV as a babysitter – there are moments when you are truly grateful for the TV but think twice before you switch it on. Is this the best use of time?
- avoid putting a TV or computer in your child's bedroom.

Remember that children under seven can be very frightened by scary things (monsters, villains, evil magicians, etc.) and telling them that they are make-believe does not help and won't console them. Children under the age of seven do not have a clear idea of what is real and what is fantasy.

Case study: Marcia aged four-and-a-half

Marcia has two older brothers aged eight and ten years. The boys are very involved with after-school activities but her parents try to set aside at least half an hour each evening to read to the three children together. Each child is allowed to choose a book and Marcia often brings two or three books that she likes. Her brothers are very happy to listen to her stories and often comment on ones they remember. Equally Marcia likes to listen to the boys' stories although her mother said she does not always follow the plot, but as she can sit with her brothers she is more than happy. She has become very knowledgeable about cars and space adventures!

The boys each have a weekly magazine and Marcia goes to the supermarket with her mum and selects one she likes (usually because of the free toy on the cover). She always gets out her magazine when she sees her brothers reading theirs.

Marcia's parents are very strict with the amount of time they allow the children to watch the TV. Marcia is restricted to 30 minutes a day and she and her mum look through the paper and decide when and what to see. Only when she has chosen is she allowed to turn on the TV.

Marcia loves books and her interests range from pop-up books, to picture books, to books about things she likes to do. She has just become interested in joke books but often does not understand them. She will ask her brothers the joke and laugh for ages when she tells them the punch line. Her great wish is that she could read like her brothers. She often says to her Grandma, 'I will read to you Grandma' and then she makes up the words to go with the pictures of the story. However, after a few minutes she says, 'But I'm not really reading.'

What has Marcia learned?
Marcia has learned that:

- books are important in her family
- there are many different kinds of books
- she can listen to a story being read and enjoy the relaxed company of her brothers even though she cannot follow the plot

- she likes some books more than others
- the words are important and for jokes you must get them right
- she can pretend to be reading but she knows she is not reading the actual words.

What is meant by the term 'Foundation Stage'?

In the UK, the DCSF (Department for Children, Schools and Families) describes the education of children from age three-and-a-half to five-and-a-half as the 'Foundation Stage'. Children may complete the Foundation Stage in a separate nursery although many children attend their local school for the foundation years.

What goes on in the Foundation Stage?

In the Foundation Stage children are taught all skills (for literacy, numeracy and social skills) through a combination of 'structured play' and more formal aspects of teaching and learning. Some parents may feel impatient for their child to make a 'proper start' with reading but research strongly supports the importance of play as a medium for learning. What might seem like undirected time to the inexperienced outsider is, in fact, a systematic programme for allowing children to explore and experiment which psychologists believe is the most advantageous start to formal learning. During this time your child's progress is being carefully monitored and the stages she has achieved are systematically recorded. This forms the basis for the more formal teaching for children aged five to six.

Under the guise of 'play' your child will be experimenting with sounds and words and linking them to letters and words. She will play games to match words and sounds and listen to rhymes and rhythms. This 'incidental learning' is not haphazard and is the essential counterpart to the direct teaching which will increasingly become a feature in your child's school life when she enters Year 1.

Hyper-parenting

In his book *Under Pressure: Rescuing Our Children from the Culture of Hyper-parenting* (2008), Carl Honoré describes parents who put excessive competitive pressure on their children (Mandarin lessons at two!) as 'hyper-parents'. It is easy to mock such extreme examples of 'pushy' parents but, in reality, it is quite difficult for parents to strike a balance between being a concerned parent and a 'hyper-parent'. Parents may well have forgotten details of their own first tentative steps into education (and, indeed, many of them would have made those steps at a later age than their own offspring). This might result in them having unrealistic expectations about what their four- or five-year-old should be achieving.

Supporting your child's learning

It is essential that you visit your child's nursery or school to find out what they are doing to introduce reading and to ask what you can do to help your child at home. Research shows that parents who support their child at home make an enormous difference to their child's educational success.

Continue reading to your child

Just because your child has started school is not a reason to discontinue book sharing times at home. The best support for your child on her journey to become a reader is to continue to read to her every day. At school she will be beginning to learn the building blocks of reading – the names of the letters, the sounds the letters make and what some words look like. These skills will only blossom in an environment where children see a purpose for the skills – to be able to read some of their favourite books that have been read to them at home.

Support the 'topic' chosen by the class teacher

Most schools have a 'topic' which lasts for approximately six weeks. This topic will be a theme such as 'families' or 'ourselves' or 'on the farm'. In the topic the teacher will explore the theme through, for example, playing games, colouring pictures, counting, cutting out, and even learning to write some letter shapes and numbers set around the theme of the farm. You could support this at home by reading books about farms.

Helping with letter formation

One of the things your child will be taught when she start school is how to write the letters of the alphabet. It is important that your child learns from the start the most efficient way of doing this so that she avoids having to re-learn the skill later on. The school will have chosen a particular style of handwriting and they may show you a chart with directional arrows which indicate how to form each letter. The school will first focus on the lower case letters (not capitals) and these are the ones you should help your child to practise. Encourage your child to hold a pencil between the thumb and long finger of her 'preferred writing hand' and to use her forefinger to steady the pencil.

> **Top tip**
>
> One way you could help your child to practise each letter shape is by writing a letter using a highlighter pen. Then invite your child to write the letter shape in pencil 'inside' the highlighter.

Helping your child with phonics

There are lots of ways you can support your child as she learns the sounds the letters make. It is always worth asking the school if there is anything specific you can do, but the games in this chapter (see page 128) will give your child a good basic knowledge of phonics in a fun, games-based way.

> **Top tip**
>
> Remember it is far more important that your child enjoys school and is happy to go there than for you to try to teach her after school. Don't turn play into lessons. If your child becomes nervous or distressed it is very important to discuss this at school to get to the bottom of the problem. An anxious child will not be in a position to learn.

What are the letter sounds?

There are 26 letters in the English alphabet but those letters (in various combinations) have to represent the 44 speech sounds that make up the English language (see Appendix 1 on page 223). One of the skills we employ when reading is that we map sounds on to the letters. Then we blend the sounds and produce the word. In school, children are taught to associate the letters with sounds. This enables them to translate the letters into sounds in order to read words and to select letters to represent sounds when attempting to spell a word. Acquiring this phonic knowledge takes children time before they are confident in most letter/sound associations.

How do schools teach phonics?

Every school has a programme for teaching these sounds to children. Some use a programme that teaches the children to associate a particular action to a sound, for example, the child might pretend to be hitting a drum with drumsticks for the sound 'd'.

Some schools set out to familiarize children with all 44 sounds as soon as possible. Children look at charts of the letters and rote learn which sounds the letters make. They may concentrate on six sounds initially and practise blending combinations of those sounds to make a variety of words, for example, tap, pat, sat, pin, nip, tin, pit, pat, tip. Most schools use a mixture of approaches and try to teach phonics as imaginatively as possible.

> **Top tip**
> Look carefully at the guidance on how to pronounce each individual sound (see Appendix 1 on page 223).

How can you help your child?

The challenging thing for parents is to strike a balance between being very engaged with their child's education and overstepping the mark. The trick is to always make the learning fun and never to let your child feel a failure. When little children experience failure it does not inspire them to try harder; it makes them feel that they are useless and they seek to avoid the situation again. Learning the sounds of the letters of the alphabet may not seem a very motivating thing to a four-year-old and the best way to engage them is to make the learning part of play.

Top tip

Spend just a few minutes each day playing phonic games. This 'little and often' approach is much better than extended periods of time which will probably only end in your child getting something wrong and feeling bad about it. The golden rule is: If your child is not enjoying the game, stop and suggest another activity that you know she enjoys.

Hearing the first sound in a word

You can help your child by:

- taking as many opportunities as you can to identify the starting letter sound in things in your child's environment. For example, finding the initial letter sound of your child's name in a street name, a place name or a shop name. Say to your child, 'I can see an "s" like at the start of your name. Can you see it? What sound does it say?'
- finding things around the house that start with the letter for a 'sound of the week'. Put these together on a table and challenge your child to find new things to add. Occasionally take away an item and see if your child can remember what is missing.
- singing songs that emphasize letter sounds, for example:
  'I'm h h h h happy,
  I sing all day long.
  I'm h h h h happy,
  Will you join my song?'
- substituting other words and letters – 'I'm m m m m merry' or 'I'm t t t t Tommy', etc.

Phonic games

All the following games can easily be adapted to more challenging games as your child becomes more confident with letter sounds.

Games to help children hear the sound at the beginning of a word

I spy

This game can be played at any time but is particularly useful in a car or on any journey. The first player looks around and says 'I spy with my little eye something beginning with the sound "a".' The other players try to guess what this could be. When a player guesses correctly that player takes over and says 'I spy …' and selects something else starting with a different letter sound.

How many can we find?

While travelling or even just sitting in a room see how many things you can see that start with a specific letter, for example, the letter 'c'. You might like to provide clues to help your child such as, 'I can see something on top of the bookcase' (clock) or 'I can see an animal sleeping under the sofa' (cat).

Granny went to market

The first player says, 'Granny went to market and she bought an apple.' The next player has to repeat the sentence but add something else that Granny could buy that starts with the same letter sound, for example, 'Granny went to market and she bought an apple and an alligator' (or ant, anchor, arrow, antelope, etc.) Children may have difficulty thinking up the words but when they have played this a couple of times they do remember the different things from previous games. As they get better you could work through the alphabet so the first player has 'a' and the next 'b', etc.

Alliteration

It is fun to try to make up sentences which have lots of things starting with the first letter of your child's name: 'Ben bought a big bear and a buffalo.'

Many children enjoy saying tongue twisters either made up or known. They laugh at the funny way they can get muddled with the words. For example: 'Which wicked witch wished a wicked wish?' or 'Six slippery snails slid slowly seaward.'

Card games for phoneme recognition

First letter snap (for two players)

You will need: 12 cards (cut from the front and back of a cereal packet), a felt-tip pen.

What to do: On six cards draw objects which all begin with one letter sound – for example, car, cat, cow, cap, cup, cake – and on the remaining six cards draw objects with a different letter sound – for example, ball, book, bell, bird, bag, box. (Commercial cards are available but they often do not have enough cards starting with the same letter sound.) You can also make and add further letter sound cards as your child becomes more familiar with different letter sounds.

Show your child the pictures and ensure she can recognize each one! Next shuffle the cards and deal them out between the players. Take it in turns to turn over a card. If both cards start with the same sound, the first player to shout 'snap' picks up all the played cards from the table.

The winner is the first player to get all the cards.

Pairs (for two players)
You will need: Use the 12 cards from the game above.

What to do: Shuffle the cards and place them face down on the table. Players take it in turns to turn over two cards. If they start with the same letter sound the player says both the words and the starting sound, and keeps the pair. If they do not make a pair turn the cards back face down in the same place.

Play continues until all the pairs have been picked up. The winner is the player with the most pairs.

Match it! (for two players)
You will need: A set of four cards, on which you have drawn objects which start with the same letter, for example: dog/door/duck/drum. Make four further sets, for example: egg/elephant/envelope/engine; fish/flower/feather/flag; goat/gate/gloves/grapes; sun/sock/sausage/snail.

What to do: Take two cards for each initial letter sound from the pack and spread them out face down on the table and then deal out the other cards between the players. Players put down any pairs they have in their hands. They must name the object (and the starting sound) and show the other player their pair. Then players take turns to turn over a card and see if it makes a pair with a picture in their hand. If so, they put the pair on the table.

If the player does not make a pair, the card is returned to the table face down. Play continues until all the pairs have been made.

The winner is the player with the most pairs.

Take away (for two players)

You will need: A tray, and cards from the game above.

What to do: Place five picture cards starting with different letter sounds on the tray and show them to the other player. Name the object and identify the starting sound for each card.

Cover the cards and remove one. Ask the other player which is the missing picture and what letter sound does it start with. When the player has correctly identified the card and the sound replace the card on the tray. The person who identifies the missing card correctly takes away the next card.

The winner is the player who gets the most cards correct.

NB Children develop at different rates with different things. Chapter 07 has a range of phonic games which extend the beginning phonics games in this chapter. If you feel your child will enjoy further phonic games then turn to page 157.

Top tip

Limit the number of cards so that your child can succeed. It is better to start with a few cards to ensure that there are plenty of chances for getting it right.

Games to help your child recognize words on sight

Twelve words make up a quarter of all the words we read, whether it is a beginning reading book or *The Times* newspaper (see Appendix 2, page 225). Fifty words make up nearly half of all the words we read, so it makes sense to familiarize children with these words as quickly as possible. These words are often described as the 'high frequency words'. The trouble is that many of these words are not easy to read by blending the sounds of the letters in sequence. They are described as 'irregular'. The best way for children to learn to recognize these words is by seeing them as whole words and memorizing them.

It is worth noting that the words themselves are not 'interesting' to a child. They are words like 'of', 'by', 'has' and 'they'. Children are much more interested in words like 'ice cream', 'party' and 'toys'! Because the high frequency words only have meaning when in the context of a story or an information book, it is important that, right from the beginning, children see words in context.

However, provided your child has many opportunities to meet these high frequency words in the context of enjoyable books then it makes sense to also draw attention to these words in isolation. Playing games with your child is an excellent way to help your child to recognize these whole words.

Common high frequency words

Here is a list of common high frequency words often used in first reading books:

a	but	had	in	no	was
an	can	has	is	not	we
and	dad	he	it	on	went
as	did	help	like	she	will
at	for	her	look	the	with
be	get	him	mum	to	yes
big	got	I	my	up	you

> **Top tip**
>
> For all the following word games, when you write the words use a clear printed handwriting style. Use lower case (except for the first letter in a sentence or a name).

Match the sentence

You will need: Thin card, scissors, a felt-tip pen or a printer.

What to do: Choose a sentence from the reading book your child brings home from school, for example, 'Biff put the book in her bag.' Either write it onto a strip of thin card or type it and print it. (**NB** The sentence should be written on one line and in large letters.)

Write the sentence exactly the same on a second strip of card. Cut up the second sentence into the separate words. Place the whole sentence strip on the table. Now give your child the separate words in the correct sentence order and ask your child to match the words to the words in the sentence strip, saying the words as she matches them.

Praise your child each time she gets it right. When your child can do this easily, give her the separate words out of sentence order. Finally, see if your child can make the sentence with the separate words without matching the words to the model sentence.

What's missing?
You will need: The cut up words from 'Match the sentence'.

What to do: Place the words face up in the correct sentence order. Read the sentence together and then tell your child to shut her eyes and remove one of the words. Close the gap. Ask your child to look at the sentence and to tell you which word is missing.

Reverse roles and ask your child to remove a word for you to work out what is missing. Praise your child when she is correct.

Cross the water
You will need: 15 pieces of A4 paper, a felt-tip pen.

What to do: Select words that you think your child knows, for example, their name, mum, dad, and, on, etc. Write each word onto a piece of paper (three times for each word) and then scatter the words onto the floor face up. Explain to your child that she is going to cross the water but she has to only jump on the word that you say. If she gets it wrong she will fall into the water.

Reverse the roles and get your child to select a word and to check that you have got it right.

NB If your child enjoys this game you can increase the number of different words but remember it is better for her to be 100 per cent successful than just 60 per cent successful but feel a failure.

Step by step
You will need: Rectangular cards with words you want your child to learn written in clear lower case print – one word per card.

What to do: Shuffle the cards and stand at one end of the room. Hold up a card. If your child can read it she may take one step forwards. Repeat with another card until your child reaches you.

Reverse roles and see if you can get to your child. (You might like to make a few mistakes for your child to correct.)

Snap

You will need: 24 cards with common words written on them (each word will need to be repeated on four cards so that there are plenty of snap opportunities). Words to use might include: 'and', 'is', 'on', 'can', 'we', 'help', 'you', etc.

What to do: Shuffle the cards and deal them out between the two players. Make it clear that the players must say the word written on the card as well as call out 'snap' if two cards match.

Players take it in turns to turn over a card. If the words are the same the first player to call out 'snap' (and say the word) gets the pair. The winner is the player with the most pairs.

Memory game

You will need: Cards from 'Snap' or other sets of words your child needs to learn.

What to do: Turn all the cards face down. Players take it in turns to turn over two cards. If they match the player must read the words and then remove the pair from the table.

If they do not match the player replaces the card face down in the same place. Play continues until all the cards have been paired. The winner is the player with the most pairs.

Top tip

Don't hesitate to ask your child's teacher if you have any concerns about your child's progress. The chances are that a quick word with the teacher will allay your fears and you can relax and enjoy your child's learning.

Frequently asked questions

Our twins (aged four-and-a-half) do not want to read to us the reading books they bring home from school. They just like me to read to them. I think the boys are bored with these first readers as they both love having exciting books read to them! What should we do to try to get them to read the books the school is sending home?

Try to read the books they're being asked to read in the most exciting and dramatic way you can. It does not matter if they hear you read the book first. You could then suggest that you all take it in turns to read a line each and see if they can also make the story exciting. Praise their attempts and show them how pleased you are when they read their books.

It is important that your boys enjoy reading and if the books do not interest them discuss this with the class teacher and ask if they have other books they might enjoy more.

If all else fails sometimes a little bribery works! This could be points towards something they want to buy or show them the kitchen timer and explain that if they can do their reading in a certain time then you will extend the time you read to them.

My son has been in school for a term. Every week he brings back some letter sounds to learn. He is very good at looking at the letter, for example, the letter 'b' and saying 'b' 'b' 'b' but when I ask him what sound he can hear at the beginning of 'but', 'book' or 'bed' he does not seem to have a clue. How can I help him?

Many children find it extremely difficult to isolate an individual sound from other sounds in the word. As adults we find it easy to separate a single sound from a word because we have a visual image in our minds of what the word looks like. Young children do not have this advantage. They have to rely entirely on their auditory memory and it takes a long time before that is 100 per cent reliable.

The first thing to do is to talk to his class teacher about your concerns and see if they would like you to do activities at home that are similar to the way the school is introducing initial letter sounds. It is also worth checking that he can recognize rhyming words. Rhyme is a larger 'chunk' of sound and it is the starting point for children to hear the difference between: 'king' and 'ring'. (See Chapter 05, page 100 for rhyming activities.)

If he can identify rhyme, then you might try to check that he understands exactly what you want him to do. There are several letters in our alphabet where you can emphasize the initial sound without distorting the letter, for example, words starting with the letters 's', 'f', 'v', 'l', 'm' and 'n'. Show him the letter and let him identify it and make the sounds. Praise him. Then explain that you are going to say some words that start with the sound 's' and extend the single sound, for example, 'sssssssssun', 'ssssssit'. Then ask him to join in with you and make the funny words. Finally, tell him again that the 's' sound is the first sound in the words. Can he tell you the first sound in 'sssssssssam'?

Try with other letters such as 'fffffffffffish', 'mmmmum' and 'nnnnno'. When you are sure that he both understands what you want him to do and he can identify the extended sound, move on to the more difficult letters that can only be made with a short sound. Don't forget to praise him and tell him how pleased you are when he gets it right. If he still has difficulty or is getting upset, talk to the teacher.

My daughter will not be five until August and she is the youngest in her class. She started Foundation in September and this term she brought back her first reading books with just one line of simple text on each page. She reads to us every day and points to the words but her pointing rarely matches the word she is saying. She obviously knows the words by heart but isn't really reading. What should I do?

It is amazing how quickly children learn to remember the words in a book – indeed most adults would love to have this ability! The teacher does not expect your child to instantly recognize all the words in the book. He or she is interested in discovering whether your daughter knows that the print is what readers look at; that she can point at the words in a left to right direction and that she expects the print to relate to the picture and to make sense.

Read the book to your child first and point very carefully at the words as you say them. Then ask her to 'read' the words and help her to point at each word. Praise her attempts.

You could play a little game with her. Write the sentence from the book onto a strip of card and cut up each word. Then lay out the sentence with good gaps between each word and read and point together. Let her point at each in turn and you say the word. Then suggest that she points at each word in turn and says each word. Do not expect her to recognize those words the next day. Recognizing words takes a long time but helping her to get more and more accurate with her saying and pointing is the beginning of the journey into reading.

My son knows all his letter sounds and when he reads a word he insists on sounding out each letter before he says the complete word despite the fact that he can recognize whole words. How can I persuade him to read the words as whole words and not sound out each letter?

Don't panic – you are not alone – many children do what your son is doing! The good news is it is only a phase and soon enough your child will realize that he does not need to spend time sounding out each separate sound but can just 'say' the word.

Why some children seem over-reliant on sounding out could be because when they know their letter sounds and they know that sounding out the letters helps them to read unfamiliar words they become hooked on using this strategy even when they could by-pass this approach and just say the word.

One strategy to try with your son is to write the words you think he can recognize onto separate small cards. Then play a game where you place them face up and whoever says the word first gets the card. (You could be a little slow off the mark but win occasionally!) When he next reads to you praise him if he reads the words you know he can recognize and point out that when you read him a story you do not need to sound out the letters. For other sight word games see page 131.

My daughter goes to a different school from her best friend. I have noticed that her friend has a reading book and is beginning to read but my daughter has not had a book yet. I am worried that my child will be behind her friend in reading. What should I do?

Schools do differ in the approaches that they use to teach children to read. It is very important that you express your concerns to your daughter's class teacher. She will explain what the school does and why the books are not sent home for the parents to practise with their child.

Just because the school doesn't send books home yet does not mean that you couldn't start preparing her for reading. You could play the phonic or sight word games suggested on pages 128–34. You should also continue reading to your daughter as that will still be the most significant means of ensuring your daughter makes a smooth transition into reading.

My daughter has a different reading book sent home every few days. These books are very easy to read and she just looks at the pictures and then says the text. She obviously knows the books by heart. Should I cover up the pictures to make her look at the print?

It is very encouraging to hear that your daughter comes home with lots of books. However, when children start to learn to read they need to rely on the pictures to give them the context and also to help 'tell' the story. Covering up the pictures and testing your daughter's knowledge of the words in the book is turning what should be an enjoyable sharing activity into a test and is unlikely to make her become a keen reader. If you do want to help her to read common words you could play some of the sight word games suggested on page 131. If you are really concerned ask her class teacher for advice.

My son just doesn't seem to be able to learn letter sounds. The school says he needs to know them before he can have a book. I am getting really worried that he will be far behind his friends. What should I do?

It is very important that you talk to his class teacher or the head teacher about your concerns. Some children do find it very difficult to attach a sound to a letter shape and it may be that he should learn to read some words as 'sight words' first. Often when a child recognizes a word they can then use this knowledge to help them decode other words. For example, if he can recognize the word 'cat' you can then show him that other words such as 'cot' and 'cup', start with the same letter but that they also contain different letters. There is no fail-safe route that guarantees reading success for all children. It is important that if one way does not seem to be working, your child should be offered another way.

Whatever you decide to do it is very important that you continue to read aloud to him and ensure that he continues to enjoy books.

Summary

- Reading to your child will provide the foundation for language development and the springboard into reading.
- Aim to read a wide range of books to your child. Make good use of your local library.
- Playing 'reading games' is an excellent way to tune your child in to the words and sounds of our language (and they're fun too!).

07

reading and your child (5–7 years)

In this chapter you will learn:
- how schools teach reading
- the place of phonics and a sight vocabulary in learning to read
- how to listen to your child read to you
- the importance of continuing to read to your child
- what is meant by a 'reading age'
- how reading is assessed
- the importance of playing reading games with your child.

The process of learning to read is extremely complex; it is a web woven of intricate designs involving cognitive, affective, social, linguistic, physical and experiential elements. All of these aspects combine in one unified whole to dynamically influence both the process and product we call reading.

D. Ray Reutzel and Robert B. Cooter Jr, *Teaching Children to Read* (2003)

The journey to becoming a reader

Between the ages of five and seven years children make amazing progress in their learning. As they begin to read they are very hesitant word readers; they read out loud with long pauses between the words and in a voice like a little robot. However, by the time they are seven-and-a-half many have become silent readers who are willing to pick up any book that they think they can read. A child's journey along this path to becoming a reader will be full of stops and starts. Some children seem to learn effortlessly while others are more plodding in their progress but may be more accurate than the 'quick' readers. Some children take longer to settle into school and find the first steps of reading difficult but may be making huge strides in other spheres of learning, for example, with social skills or learning to work independently and to persevere with a task.

Children aged five and over who have been read to, who enjoy looking through books and who are becoming curious about the printed word are ready to learn to read. They already know lots of things that readers do. They know:

- the right way to hold a book
- how to turn the pages in order
- that illustrations and photographs are clues to the content of the book
- that in English you read from the top of the page to the bottom and from left to right
- that words you say can be represented in print
- that letters represent sounds and that sounds make up the word
- that there are different kinds of books, some fascinating, some funny, some sad
- that reading is important and worthwhile.

When they reach the end of the year in which they are seven most children will be able to read hundreds of words and write in sentences.

This journey is not smooth for any child. Some days when you listen to them read you will be thinking how well they are doing and then, the following week, it seems as if they have forgotten everything they had learned and they are stumbling over words they knew perfectly well the week before. Sometimes you can almost see the progress they are making from day to day, but at other times it seems they have been standing still for ages.

How difficult is it to read?

Most of us have forgotten how we learned to read and so we imagine it was an easier skill to acquire than it was. To appreciate how difficult it is to learn to read try to read the following passage. It has been printed in 'mirror writing'. That is, the letters are printed back to front. This has the effect of making the letters look unfamiliar and so you will be trying to read in much the same way as your child is, and you will have to sort out every letter and then put a sound to the letter (or letters) and then blend the sounds and work out the word. As you read try to remember what things gave you problems.

Mirror writing

Learning to read is not easy. Although a great deal of research has been undertaken into how children learn to read this by no means guarantees that all children will become readers effortlessly. What research does reveal is that it is essential for children to understand that the reason for learning to read is for them to get meaning from texts. If parents demonstrate the pleasure they get from reading and if they support their child's reading in a happy and relaxed situation, they can have an enormous impact on their child's journey to reading.

(See Appendix 3, page 226 for a printed version of this text the right way round.)

How did you get on?

Like your child starting with reading, you had to know quite a lot about reading in order to even try to read the passage. You had to know:

- which way to go along the line of print
- where to start reading
- that the white spaces between the print show you where one word ends and another begins
- that letter shapes are a clue to the letter sound
- that printed text (usually!) makes sense. Even if you managed to decode the words, did you manage to understand what you were reading?

So what did you find difficult?

- Were some letters easily muddled, such as b/d, f/t, n/u?
- Were some words difficult to decode, such as 'easy' and 'guaranteed'?
- Was it easy to lose the thread of what you were reading about?
- Did you feel as if your eyes were getting tired?
- Did you not really want to continue reading?
- Did you read slower and slower as you went through the text?

A little exercise like this is a very good way to put adults in the position of the child learning to read. It helps us appreciate how difficult reading is. Many of the difficulties you faced (including those about wanting to give up altogether!) are likely to be the same as your child experiences as he begins to learn to read.

What help would you have liked?

- Would you have liked someone sitting beside you who you knew could read the passage effortlessly and who you sensed was getting impatient with your slow progress?
- Would you have liked someone to keep interrupting you saying things like 'Sound it out' or 'You had that word last week' or 'That's an easy one'?
- Or would it have helped if you had had a good reader to support you who encouraged you and did not get impatient as you tried to work out each word?

Well, in a nutshell, that last point describes the role of the supportive parent as a child learns to read!

How is reading taught?

> *Reading is much more than the decoding of black marks upon a page: it is a quest for meaning and one which requires the reader to be an active participant.*

> (Cox Report, 1989)

Each school is responsible for providing books and materials to help children to learn to read, but the choice of the books and the way the school uses these is unique to every school. However, schools do have many things in common.

No school will be exactly the same as another in the way that they teach reading, but all schools want to make the introduction of reading as simple and as enjoyable as possible. It is very important that you understand what your school does and that you and your child work together in harmony with the school.

Successful reading depends on learning to use a range of strategies – word recognition, phonic knowledge, using the context and using knowledge of grammar – and each of these strategies is equally important. The way in which schools decide to teach the strategies is the choice of the school but most schools use a combination of methods.

What is phonics?

Phonics is the ability to link letter sounds to letter shapes. When we come across a word we have not seen before, we use our knowledge of phonics to decode the word and make an informed guess at how it should be pronounced. In many cases, we then realize that the word is one we have heard before and we know what it means. This is what happens to children when they start to read – they know what a dog is, they have heard the word 'dog' but they have not tried to *read* the word before so they sound it out, letter by letter, and then by blending the sounds together they 'read' the word. This means that readers (young and old) can decode words they do not immediately recognize. Of course, once they have seen a word many times, they no longer need to use phonics to decode it – it becomes a word they recognize on sight.

Teaching reading using phonics

Experts agree that all children need careful, systematic and imaginative teaching of phonics. That is, helping children to hear and recognize the separate sounds in each word. Each separate speech sound is called a 'phoneme'. There are 44 phonemes in the English language. Every word in English is made up from a combination of these sounds.

The skill of identifying individual sounds in words relies on some very accurate hearing indeed. When teaching reading using phonics, teachers require children to listen to the tiny differences between the individual letter sounds. Some children find this very difficult.

In the classroom, children are taught the sounds of the letters and letter combinations (see Appendix 1, page 223) as quickly as possible. Teachers generally introduce the children to the name of the letter, demonstrate how it is written (called a 'grapheme'), and then they teach the sound of the letter or combination of letters (phonemes). For example:

the name of the letter 'a' is 'ay'
it is written '**a**' (the grapheme)
the sound of the letter (phoneme) is 'a' as in apple

When children can recognize and say the correct sounds to the shapes of the letters they are then taught how to blend the sounds to make a word, for example, h/a/t.

(See Chapter 06, page 127 for a brief overview of the different phonic programmes used in schools.)

Top tip

Ask the school how they are teaching letter sounds and what they would like you to do to help your child to learn the sounds.

Teaching reading using whole word recognition

Some schools teach children to recognize on sight a number of words that occur very frequently in our language. These words are called 'high frequency words', such as: 'I', 'am', 'here', 'is' and 'a' (see Appendix 2, page 225). Children are shown these words in the context of a sentence, for example, 'Here is a cat' (under a picture of a cat). Then the children are given a card with the word 'is' on it and they are asked to match the word with the word in the sentence. Later they may be shown the card with the word 'is' and asked if they can remember what the word is. When the children can recognize enough words they can read the whole sentence. From this start of recognizing the whole word, teachers help the children to learn the letter sound of each letter by segmenting each word into its separate sounds (phonemes). When a child can recognize the word 'cat' he is then encouraged to segment the word into its three phonemes c/a/t. This is called 'decoding' a word.

Which method is best – phonics or word recognition?

In truth, children need to be able to do both skills – break down words into their separate phonemes and recognize some words as complete words – and most schools use a combination of these two approaches. So schools may ask a parent to help their child to make sounds to specific letters while also asking them to encourage the child to recognize and read high frequency words.

It has to make sense

To become proficient readers and spellers children need to learn both how to blend letter sounds to make a word and how to segment a word into its constituent sounds in order to write the word. But this is only part of the reading process. It is of the utmost importance that children realize that the reason for reading is to make sense of the printed word. Some children become very adept at recognizing the words and can read at a rapid rate, but all they are doing is recognizing the words, they are not seeking to understand what the words mean. So whatever method the school uses to teach initial reading the approach has to be underpinned by ensuring the child reads to make sense of the words.

This is where all the early work of reading to your pre-school child will pay dividends. Children who have been regularly read to will have a good understanding of the grammar of the English language and this will help them to get meaning from texts. When they misread a word they will 'hear' that it is not making sense and stop to reconsider what the text is saying. Children who are 'word' readers often fail to notice that their reading is not making sense. For example, a child might read: 'The house was running round the field' (misreading 'house' for 'horse') and not stop and think that the sentence doesn't make sense.

One of the roles of parents supporting their child's reading at home is to ensure that he is thinking about the meaning of what he is reading. If a mistake that doesn't make sense occurs we can quietly say: 'Oh! Does that sound right? Let's look at that sentence again.'

Reading schemes

What is a reading scheme?

A reading scheme is a series of carefully graded books that enable the beginner reader to practise the skills of reading. A reading scheme may have fiction and non-fiction texts.

Some reading schemes are based on the phonic approach to reading and these texts will have simple phonically decodable words where children blend the sounds to read the words.

Other reading schemes are based on the repetition of high frequency words (see Appendix 2, page 225). These words will be introduced very gradually and repeated in the text as often as possible.

Many reading schemes use a combination of a phonic approach to teaching reading and a high frequency words approach. So that in a predominantly phonic scheme most of the words will be phonically regular (that is, each letter has a separate sound such as c/a/t), but there will be some high frequency words which are not phonically regular such as the word 'said' which has four letters but only three sounds.

As the children get better at reading so the higher levels of the scheme become more challenging. What all schemes have in common is that they have been carefully graded so that the child makes small and hopefully successful steps up the scheme.

Do schools use just one reading scheme?

Some schools select one particular scheme to be their main scheme. This scheme may have a core of characters that the children meet in every level. Other reading schemes introduce different characters in each book.

Many schools do not use just one reading scheme. They prefer to offer children as wide a range of books as possible. They select the 'best' from many different reading schemes.

How are the levels of difficulty indicated?

Educational publishers indicate the steps of progress in different ways. Some use colour coding on the cover of each book, for example, pink = level one; red = level two. Other publishers use numbers to indicate the level of difficulty. If the scheme is colour coded, the colours chosen will not necessarily be the same choice as another scheme produced by a different publisher.

Schools that use a number of different reading schemes grade all the books into levels of difficulty. Some schools use coloured stickers and put these on the covers of the books. These colours may not match the colours selected by the publishers.

Reading scheme races!

Young children are rarely competitive, especially with school work, but when a child begins to learn to read many parents become anxious about the rate at which their child is progressing and begin to compare this with that of their friend's children. They will check to see if their child is on the same level and if they think he is behind they try to increase the pressure on their child to do more. Often the first questions they ask as their child runs to meet them in the playground are 'What reading book have you got? What "colour" is it? What colour is Holly's book?' They do not intend to put pressure on their child but children are very quick to pick up on any hint of disappointment. Instead of reading becoming something children want to share with their parents it becomes a time they start to dread and they begin to worry that they are not doing as well as their parents want them to.

Remember that your child is unique and will respond to ways of teaching differently from his siblings or peers. However, time is a great leveller and by the time they are ten years old some children who have appeared to be slower than others at the beginning of their school lives have generally 'caught up' if not surpassed those who seemed to make such a rapid start with reading.

Like many things in childhood, starting early is not necessarily a sign that the child will be more skilful later on. Parents may boast about how quickly their child learned to walk, but early walking does not mean that the child will grow into an adult who has above average walking skills!

In her informative book *Reading Magic* (2001), Mem Fox says that one reason why TV is so popular with children is that it isn't competitive. We don't talk about a good TV watcher or a bad TV watcher. We couldn't imagine even the most pushy parent claiming in the playground: 'Fiona is in the top television-watching group.' Reading, by contrast, can be so competitive. Every child (and more importantly, every parent) knows exactly who's on what level. So for children, learning to read can become associated with fear, shame and boredom. No wonder they prefer television.

Parents would do well to follow the advice of the children's author Hiawyn Oram in her poem 'Urgent Note to my Parents':

> Don't ask me to do what I can't do.
> Only ask me to do what I can.
> Don't ask me to be what I can't be.
> Only ask me to be what I am.
> Don't one minute say 'Be a big girl.'
> And the next – 'You're too big for that!'
> Please, don't ask me to be where I can't be.
> Please be happy with right where I'm at!

How to listen to your child read to you

It is very important to share your child's book and to listen to him read it as often as possible but do not make this session last too long. It is far better to spend a few minutes each day rather than 30 minutes once or twice a week. Choose a time to hear your child read that suits you and your child. If possible make this a regular slot so that your child knows when it is coming up.

Remember that your child has had a pretty exhausting day at school and to come home and to have to start to 'work' again may not be very popular. Try to keep the session as relaxed as possible. If on occasions, your child really does not want to read his school book, then give him a night off and read it to him. (You might even be able to coax him to read the occasional page once you have started reading.)

Top tip

Put a timer on for about ten minutes or the time you want to spend reading, and explain that this is as long as you will work together. If you do have longer and you are both enjoying the book carry on, but achieving ten minutes four or five times a week is good going.

Before sharing his reading book settle yourselves down and try to ensure that it is quiet and peaceful.

- Let your child hold the book and turn the pages.
- Look at the book together and talk about the pictures. This is very important because when children start to read it should be an understanding of the text that leads the reading. When children have to stop to work out (or remember) quite a number of the words on each page, it is easy for them to lose the thread of what the text is about.
- As you talk about the pictures, use the nouns that are in the text. These are likely to be new words for your child to decode but if you have used them in context as you discuss the picture that will help him to remember them.
- Ensure that your child understands the words. Sometimes a word can be used in an unusual context, for example, 'floating' is usually associated with things floating on water but snow can also float down through the air and this might muddle your child.
- Ask if he would like you to read a few pages first.

A strategy for hearing your child read in three simple steps is: **pause, prompt** and **praise**.

As your child reads to you, listen carefully to how accurately he is reading. If he gets stuck on a word, do not immediately say the word for him but **pause** to give him a little thinking time before you intervene to help. If he manages to get the word himself, he will remember that word the next time it occurs, but if you have told him the word he will expect you to do the same next time.

If, after waiting for a few seconds, your child is still not able to work out the word then the next step is to **prompt** him.

- You might suggest he looks at the first letter and says the sound. That might trigger what the word might be.
- You might read up to the problem word again so that he hears the context of the word.
- You could suggest he leaves out the word and carries on reading to see if that triggers the missing word.

If none of these helps, tell him the word and carry on listening to him.

Remember to **praise** your child:

- when he reads correctly
- when he works out a word for himself
- when he gets to the end of a page
- when he gets to the end of the story.

Top tip

It is just as important to talk about the story as it is to hear your child read. You might start by saying what you liked about the story and encourage him to say which bits he liked or thought funny or interesting. You could talk about the pictures or the characters or think what might happen next if the story continued.

Another top tip!

At the beginning of each week try to work out what time and what days you can hear your child read. Do not feel guilty if this does not happen every day or if you forget!

Case study: Ella aged six

Ella's father read her stories every day and many of these were the traditional tales from their culture. Ella's first language is English but her father also tried to speak to her in Senegalese so she can communicate with her grandparents who speak very little English. Ella goes to after-school club four days a week as her dad cannot pick her up until 6.00 p.m.

Ella learned to read quite quickly and she used to love to sit with her dad and read to him. He tried to hear her read every day but sometimes there was only time for either Ella to read to him, or for him to read to her. Her father tried to balance out which activity took priority but mostly he thought it was better to hear Ella read. He always asked what books her friends were reading and became anxious when he heard they were on a higher level. He was determined to ensure that Ella did as well as her friends and would sometimes insist that she read her book several times until it was word perfect before she went to sleep.

He was careful to always praise Ella if she got it right but gradually Ella started to leave the reading book at school, saying she had forgotten it. Sometimes she even said she had lost it!

The school asked to have a chat with Ella's dad and explained that Ella's reading was very good but that recently she had refused to try to read any words that she was uncertain about – she only wanted to read words that she knew and she did not seem as keen to read as she had been. Her dad agreed that he had tried to make sure that Ella knew every word of her school book. The teacher explained that the mistakes children make when reading are an insight for the teacher to learn exactly which skills a child has acquired and which they are still working on. If children become anxious and only want to read if they can get every word right the first time, this will slow down their progress in reading. The teacher suggested that Ella's dad went back to making their reading sessions at home as much fun as possible. She advised him to spend more of their precious reading time reading to Ella and said that for a little time the school would send home reading books that Ella could read easily. She asked Ella's dad to help Ella to read with more intonation and expression. The teacher felt confident that this would encourage Ella into being confident enough to tackle unknown words. Ella's dad agreed and soon Ella was bringing back her reading book and showing her father what she did if she found a word a bit difficult. At the class review session later that term Ella's dad told her teacher that he was really pleased with Ella's progress and that he was getting very good at listening to her and sharing books together.

What should I do if my child finds the books too easy?

It is most likely that the books that your child brings home are ones that he has already read to an adult in school. So it might seem to you that the book is too 'easy' (if by that you mean he can remember each word quickly without having to stop to work it out) but what he is doing is showing you how well he remembers what he was taught in school.

In school your child is taught to read. At home he needs to practise reading to develop fluency and pace. This is best achieved with a text that has first been introduced to your child.

If you feel that your child is frustrated by the lack of challenge in the book he brings home to read to you, then have a chat with his class teacher. She may well be able to put your mind at rest as she may have a 'cunning plan' to ensure your child shines in front of you at home as that is the best tonic for fostering successful readers!

Does it matter if he is just remembering what the words are?

When children start to read they can often remember the whole text by heart. They look at the picture and then 'read' the words when, in fact, they are not even looking at the words at all! Don't underestimate how clever your child is being. Remembering the words on a page is no mean feat and we should not consider it 'cheating'! It is often a phase that young readers go through and they soon grow out of it.

Top tip

One way to help your child focus on the printed word is to ask him to point with his finger at the words as he says them. This can stop him thinking that reading is just remembering.

Should I cover up the pictures so he doesn't 'cheat'?

Sometimes parents think that if they cover up the pictures it will make their child look at the words but when children are starting to read, the pictures are a helpful clue to the nouns. The nouns in the text are not the priority words for your child to concentrate on. For example, if the words below the picture say 'He put it in the dustbin.' the teacher is really interested in whether your child can accurately read 'He put it in the ...' These are the key high frequency words that your child needs to learn to recognize as quickly as possible. The word 'dustbin' may not appear again in a book (perhaps for five years!) so the fact that your child can 'read' it courtesy of the picture is a good thing. It keeps the flow of the sentence going and enables your child to have a better sense of what is going on in the story.

Top tip

Many schools have a home-school booklet in which they ask teachers, parents and children to comment on the book the child is reading. The teacher checks this book frequently and if no comment has been put against a title they could presume that the parent did not have time to listen to their child that evening. The same book will therefore be sent home again. If possible make a brief remark or draw a smiley face to let the teacher know that you have shared the book.

What should I do if I think the books are too hard?

The first thing to do is to talk to your child's teacher. Explain why you think your child is not succeeding. Are you having to help him with most of the words? Does he seem unable to understand what he is reading? Is he reluctant to read or always suggests something else to do rather than read? There can be many reasons why a child is finding reading difficult:

• Some children do not really like stories and blossom when given non-fiction.
• Some children do not like the characters in the school reading scheme but make great progress when given traditional tales to read.
• Some children need more repetition of the high frequency words and succeed when the reading scheme has more structure.
• Some children like to be able to decode every word and thrive on more structured phonic readers.

It is important to tell the school early on about your concerns so that intervention is quick and effective. Waiting because you do not want to make a fuss can mean that the problem will take much longer to overcome.

NB Some reading difficulties can be more challenging to overcome (see Chapter 09, 'Children who find reading difficult').

> **Top tip**
>
> If your school has a home-school record booklet, write down your concerns as soon as you can. It is often easier to write something rather than to talk face to face – especially if you feel it is really a minor worry and seeing the teacher might look as if you were making too much of a fuss.

How do schools assess reading?

All schools have to keep careful records of a child's progress in reading and number work. They have on-going assessment records where the teacher records which books your child has read, the level of the books and the confidence of your child's reading. Periodically through the school year they will undertake a more detailed analysis of your child's reading, looking at what strategies your child uses to read 'problem' words and how well your child understands what he is reading. At the end of a school year they may use a published reading test to see if this agrees with their own assessment. Some published tests report the result as a 'reading age' while others talk about the 'percentile' your child is on.

What is a 'reading age'?

A reading age is the age at which average children can read a text of a certain difficulty. So if a child is aged six years and has a reading age of 6.0 years then his reading ability is the same as the vast majority of children aged six. If he has a reading age of 6.6 years then he is reading just above the average for the country.

What is a percentile?

Many publishers feel reporting a result as a percentile is a more accurate form of describing how well a child can read. This is based on the claim that average children of a certain age will achieve 100 per cent. If the child is above average the percentile would be a number of points above 100 and if the child was slightly below average the percentile would be under 100. Using percentages instead of months gives a more precise result – although it should be remembered that a child's performance on a standardized test can vary from day to day.

Case study: Max aged seven

Max is enjoying learning to read. He is happy to share books with his teacher and his parents and has made steady progress up the reading scheme that the school uses to level the books. He was especially happy when he had a non-fiction book to read and loved collecting facts to tell his parents. At the end of the school year he was given a reading test and this was recorded in his school report. His parents were dismayed to see that although the teacher had said how pleased he was with his progress the test result showed that his reading age was just below his chronological age.

They asked about this at the end of term parents' evening and said that they would pay for him to have extra tuition in reading over the summer holidays. His teacher assured his parents that there really was no need to worry. The test was given on just one day and the subject matter of the test was a story about two children on a trip to the seaside. The teacher pointed out that if it had been about tigers Max would probably have got a reading age well above his chronological age! The school felt that it had to give the parents the results of any tests but that their on-going teacher assessments showed that Max was a confident and proficient reader for his age and that their assessment has been based over a long period of time and not just on one hour of one day. They asked his parents to encourage Max to read as many books as possible over the school holidays and mentioned the library challenge where children got reward stickers when they had read a book and a 'super reward' if they read over a certain number.

The importance of reading to your child

As children start to read for themselves there is a tendency for parents to read less to their children. The pressures of hearing them read, getting them to the various clubs and also getting them to bed at a reasonable time seem to leave little time free for reading to them.

However, unless children have books read to them that go far beyond their reading ability they are unlikely to glimpse the real reason for reading and fail to understand that books are there waiting to be enjoyed, to impart information and to offer the opportunity of entering another world. If they begin to think that reading is a ladder to climb and that the real purpose is to be able to get to the top and then they can stop reading, they will not experience the real power of books.

Books develop empathy

It is through books that children can vicariously experience joy and sorrow, laughter and even fear. It is through books that many delicate situations can be explored and discussed and where children can come to understand the problems of others.

Books widen vocabulary

Reading books to your child is also one of the best ways to help your child acquire a wider vocabulary. When children hear the rich language of books they begin to absorb that language and in turn become clear communicators. Most English speaking adults have a vocabulary of around 12,000 to 20,000 words but the number of words they use is limited to a 'working' vocabulary of between 3,000 and 3,500 words. These words are those they use in everyday situations and the words are so often repeated throughout a year that adults do not have to stop to think whether there is a better word or a more accurate word to use. In order to acquire a wider vocabulary, adults have to hear or read new words. It is the same for children – they will pick up new language by hearing how others express themselves and the fastest and most lasting way to do this is to have good books read to them.

Joke books

At around the age of six, some children become hooked on simple jokes. Sometimes they just seem to like the fact that they can ask you a question and tell you the answer without really understanding why it is funny. Enjoying jokes can be a sign that your child is enjoying words and discovering that words can have two or more meanings. For example:

Question: 'What's got a bottom at the top?'
Answer: 'A leg!'

Literacy games

One easy way for parents to help their child with early reading skills is to play literacy games with them. **NB** Some of these games are more challenging versions of games listed at the end of Chapter 06 (see page 128).

Phonic Games

Rhyme

One excellent way to help your child tune in to the sounds in our language is to play around with rhyming words, by singing rhyming songs and playing rhyming games (see Chapter 05, page 100). Two words which rhyme have a chunk of sound at the end of each word in common. Children usually find it easier to hear this sound than to hear an individual phoneme. That is why rhyme is a very good starting point for phonics.

Encouraging your child to notice when words rhyme (and when they don't) helps him to listen to words and to distinguish what sounds words have in common. For example, recognizing that 'fish' and dish' have 'ish' in common also helps children to begin to understand that the difference between the two words are the phonemes 'd' and 'f'.

Individual letter sounds

Encourage your child to link sounds and letters (see Appendix 1, page 223). Use print in the world around you as a way of drawing your child's attention to letters and sounds. Make it into a game, for example, perhaps your street name shares a

letter with your child's name or a bus has an advert that starts
with a letter he has been practising.

On a car journey

Point out the letters or a letter from a car registration and play
a game where each passenger has to think of words that start
with the sound that that letter makes. As your child improves,
challenge yourselves to try to think of three, five or ten words
that start with that sound.

I spy

This is a familiar way to keep children occupied while waiting
for an appointment or passing the time on a long journey. One
member of the family says 'I spy with my little eye something
beginning with ...' (and chooses a letter sound). The rest of the
players have to guess what object that person is thinking of
(beginning with the chosen sound) until a player guesses
correctly. That player then becomes the 'spyer'.

Alphabet zoo

Start an alphabet sequence story by saying 'I went to the zoo
and I saw an ant.' The next player has to repeat the first
sentence but then add an animal that starts with the sound 'b'.
('I went to the zoo and I saw an ant and a bee.') Continue for as
long as you can – but encourage the children to think of the
letter 'sound' rather than the letter name, for example,
'antelope' rather than 'ape'.

Make an alphabet collage

Write the letters of the alphabet on a long strip of paper. Browse
through a shop catalogue and see if your child can find things
for each letter. He should cut out the item and stick it under the
appropriate letter.

Soldier on the bridge

You start by being the soldier and stand with your arms by your
sides. Your child asks if he can pass through the 'gate' by saying,
'Please may I pass?' You reply, 'You can pass if you can say a
word beginning with the sound ...' If he gives a correct answer
you lift your arm parallel with your shoulder and he can march
underneath. When he has done this he becomes the soldier and
won't let you pass unless you can say a word beginning with the
sound ...

Digraphs

When children know the sound of individual letters, you can then move on to recognizing those phonemes which need more than one letter to make one sound. Consonant digraphs are when two consonants make one phoneme, for example, 'sh' as in 'ship'. Vowel digraphs are when two vowels make one phoneme (see Appendix 1, page 223).

Same but different

The sound 'A' can be made with 'ai' (as in the word 'train'); 'ay' (as in the word 'day') and 'a-e' (as in the word 'make') and on rare occasions with 'ei' (as in the words 'eight'). (For further letter combinations see Appendix 1, page 223.)

On a piece of paper draw three columns. Put 'ai', 'ay' or 'a-e' at the top of one of the columns. After you have heard your child read, choose a couple of pages from the book and encourage your child to scan the words on the page to see if there are any that could be added to the columns. For example:

ai	ay	a-e
tail	day	make
rain	play	sale
wait	say	race
		page

Check that your child understands that the 'A' sound is the same but it is made with different letters in each column.

Phoneme race

You will need: A4 card, a felt-tip pen, a dice and a collection of counters.

What to do: Draw a grid of 6 x 4 squares onto a sheet of A4 card. In each square write a word which has a long vowel sound in it (see Appendix 1, page 226).

Players take it in turns to throw a dice and move the appropriate number of squares (along the bottom row from left to right and then back across the second row from right to left, etc.). When they land on a square they have to think of a word which has the same long vowel in it. If they are correct they take a counter. The winner is the first player to collect ten counters.

Turn around

What you need: Cardboard for making cards, a felt-tip pen.

What to do: Cut out 24 small cards. On five sets of four cards write words which have the same long vowel phoneme. For example:

rain may take came
feet heat me he
boat so grow show
night like my bite
blue moon fruit cute

Write 'choose a sound' on the remaining four cards. Shuffle the cards and deal out six cards to each player. Players look at their cards. (They can hold them in their hands or lay them face up on the table in front of them.)

The first player chooses a card and lays it down in the centre of the table. The next player looks at her cards and if possible puts down a card with the same phoneme sound, saying the sound as she does so. She puts this down on top of the first player's card. If the player does not have a phoneme card she can put down a 'choose another sound' card and then selects another phoneme card from her hand. If she does not have a 'choose another sound' card she picks up a card from the left over pile and play moves on to the next player.

The next player looks at his hand and sees if he can place a card with the same phoneme sound onto the cards in the middle. If not he follows the same procedure as above. The winner is the first player to get rid of all their cards.

Sight word games

Appendix 2 (page 225) lists 100 high frequency words which are the most commonly written words in the English language. Because these words occur so frequently, it is important that children learn to read them as quickly as possible. However, some of these words do not have a simple match between the letters in the word and the sounds the letters make. For example, the word 'said' is a very frequently used word (occurring in many beginning reading books) but phonically it is a very tricky word because the 'e' sound in the middle of 'said' is made with the letters 'ai'.

Some schools send home a list of frequently used words and encourage parents to support their child's learning of the words. One of the best (and most fun!) ways to learn these words is to make them into simple games.

Games to support the reading of 'tricky' words

Same or different

You will need: A sheet of A4 thin card, a felt-tip pen, a dice and counters (these can just be bits of paper or dried beans, etc.).

What to do: This game encourages children to look closely at small differences between words. Divide the card into three columns down the page and six rows across. Number the rows 1–6. In each set of three columns write two words the same and one slightly different, for example:

1. cat   cat   hat
2. man   men   man
3. and   ant   ant
4. but   cut   cut
5. no   on   no
6. am   am   an

Players take it in turns to throw the dice and then try to find the different word in the line that corresponds to the number on the dice. Each time they are correct, they take a counter. The winner is the first player to get five counters.

Read my sentence

You will need: Strips of thin card for sentences, a felt-tip pen.

What to do: On a strip of card, write a sentence (choose a sentence from your child's reading book). Make two copies. Write a number on the back of each word in the sentence and repeat with the same numbers on the second card.

If the sentence has a noun that can be illustrated draw a small picture in the corner of the card above the picture, for example, 'ball', 'fish' or 'dog'. Cut up the second sentence card into separate words. Store the sentence and the cards together in a mini plastic bag.

Show your child the sentence card and read each word pointing with your finger as you read. Ask your child to say the words with you.

Give your child the separate words that make the sentence and ask him to match them to the sentence on the sentence card. He should place each matching word below the word in the sentence. Ask him to read the sentence again. Praise correct reading.

Now shuffle the cards and ask your child to match them to the whole sentence (do this several times). Take away the sentence then say the sentence to your child and ask him to put the words in the correct order to make the sentence.

Ask your child to read the sentence he has made. Point at one or two words and challenge your child to read them. Shuffle the cards again and ask your child to make the sentence, reading each word as he puts it in place.

Top tip

Always praise your child when he gets something right. If he gets it wrong, for example, not matching all the words correctly, say, 'You're nearly right. This word is right and so is this one but let's look again at this one. Look closely. Does it match the word in the sentence? Let's try again.' If you make your child feel a failure in any part of a literacy game he will not be willing to play games with you in the future and you have lost an invaluable way to help him with reading skills.

Make a sentence card game

You will need: The word cards made from the 'Read my sentence' game (above) and some counters.

What to do: Give each player four cards. The first player can start if she has a word starting with a capital letter. She must say the word and put it down on the table and take a counter. The next player adds a word to the first one on the table so long as it makes sense, for example, 'Here is ....' but not 'Here this ... ' The player takes a counter.

If she cannot continue a sentence she can either start a new sentence with a word with a capital letter and receive a counter or take a card from the pile.

Play continues with each player receiving a counter each time they add an appropriate word to a sentence that has been started. The game ends when all the words are exhausted. The winner is the player with the most counters.

Pairs

You will need: A sheet of A4 thin card, a felt-tip pen. Select about five words from those listed in Appendix 2, page 225.

What to do: Cut out ten small cards and write each word onto two cards. Place the cards face down and take it in turns to turn over two cards. The players must read each card that they turn over. If they make a pair they keep the cards; if not, they turn them back face down in the same place and the next player has a turn. The winner is the player with the most pairs.

NB Do not select too many cards to start with and always include some words that you know your child can recognize instantly and just a couple that he is a little uncertain about.

Snap

What you need: The same cards can be used from the game above.

What to do: Players should sit next to each other so that the words are seen the right way up. Shuffle the cards and deal them out between the two players.

Players take it in turns to turn over a card. When they see two words that match they have to call out the word to win. The winner then picks up any cards on the table. Play continues until one player has all the cards.

Snakes and ladders

You will need: Word cards from any of the previous games, some counters and a board from any commercial 'Snakes and ladders' game.

What to do: Write a number 1–4 in the corner of each card. Place the cards in a pile, face down, between the players. Instead of using a dice, players take it in turns to turn over a card.

Players must read the card and move the number of places indicated on the card. If a child is successful he can move double the number but an adult can only move the number on the card.

As in snakes and ladders, if you land on a ladder you go to the top of the ladder and if you land on the head of a snake you have to go down to its tail. The winner is the first player to get 'home'.

Missing word game

You will need: Counters (dried beans or even pieces of paper will do), sentences from 'Read my sentence' (above) but written onto a strip of card omitting one word, and small word cards for each of the missing words.

What to do: Sit the players side by side so that they can see the sentences the correct way up. Put all the sentences face up on the table. Put the pile of word cards down between the players.

Players take it in turns to take a word card and to see if they can put it into one of the sentences so that it makes sense. If correct, the player takes a counter. If the player cannot use the word it is returned to the bottom of the pile and the next player has a turn. The winner is the player who has the most counters.

TV and computers

After a busy day at school many children turn to the computer or the TV as soon as they return home. Children's television programmes are often motivating and informative so it may seem perverse to suggest that TV viewing time should be strictly limited but if your child is spending a high percentage of his leisure time watching TV (no matter how 'educational' the programme may claim to be) then he is unlikely to be making the best use of his time.

Winding down after a hectic time at school by watching the TV or playing a computer game is entirely understandable, but this passive viewing really should not last longer than 30 minutes at a stretch. Even then, if you want your child to get the most out of these programmes, it is advisable that you watch or play (the computer) with him. Then, because you are involved, you can also decide a suitable stopping point.

All research into children over the age of five recommends that watching any screen needs to be limited and controlled (a suggestion of a maximum of two hours in any 24 hours is often quoted, and it is surprising how quickly this time adds up). All agree that it should not be part of the general background scene of the home. Leaving the TV or computer on, even if your child is not actively watching, would be counted as part of the two hours. Turning it off during meals, when other children come to play or when a programme ends should be something that children come to expect and accept. Using turning off the TV or computer as a threat for poor behaviour is very tempting but this generally makes it seem even more important to your child.

It is often only when we go on holiday and find that the TV is rarely used that we appreciate that it is not as essential as we or our children had thought. Many a parent has been heard to say, 'If only we did not have a TV I could really help my child with reading/number work, etc.' Remember: there is an off switch and perhaps we should get used to using it more often.

Frequently asked questions

My five-and-a-half-year-old daughter is reading really well but when she looks at a sentence and sees a long word that she thinks she cannot read she will not make any attempt to read it but just says, 'I can't read that word.' She sometimes gets books with much smaller print size in them and she has the same reaction. We have tried to persuade her to try to read the words and have shown her that she knows the words, however small the print is, but it is a battle that she seems to win most days! What should we do?

The words your daughter needs to begin to recognize are the high frequency words. Many of these are phonically regular or generally have fewer than five letters in them. The long words she is worried about are most likely to be nouns and these are usually picture-cued, that is, they are portrayed in the illustration. It is not expected that your daughter would be able to recognize these words so she is right when she says, 'I can't read that word.' Explain to her that you will help her with these words and show her how the pictures can help her. If possible, point out that the dragon in the picture and the word 'dragon' (that she said was too hard for her) start with the sound 'd'. Gradually she will begin to see that these words are achievable and she will use both the picture cue and the letter cues to help her.

It is interesting that she thinks small print is also a sign of difficulty. When she comes home with a 'small print' book suggest that you start the reading and ask her to point at the words with her finger. She will quickly come to realize that she can read these words and will be very proud when she does so.

My son is five-and-a-half. The school have sent home three A4 sheets of words (12 words on each sheet) which we have been asked to help our son to read. I have stuck them to the wall in the kitchen and at every opportunity I try to get him to recognize the words but he is making very slow progress. The words do not make any sense on their own (they are words like has, by, out) and although I have tried to help him by telling him to blend the sounds to read the words, he just doesn't seem to get it. What should I do to help him?

It is very difficult to read words out of context and lists of unconnected words are very daunting for new readers. When you are reading a book to your son, point out any of 'his' words that crop up on the page. Read the sentence with his word in it and ask him to find it. As he gets more confident you will be surprised at how many words he does begin to recognize.

If possible ask the teacher which words you should start with – are some of them easier than others or are they important words that will be needed in his reading book? Select two or three of the 'easy' or 'important' words and write them in simple sentences. Display the sentences on your kitchen wall and help your son to read them. Cut out your chosen words from the A4 sheet and place these near the sentence. Ask your son if he can find the word in the sentence and praise him when he is successful. Play a game and say you are going to change the order of the sentences on the wall and see if he can still find the words. Finally, say you are going to remove the sentences and see if he can remember what the words are. Lavish him with praise if he can do this! When he is confident with the first few words, select another couple of words to add and write more sentences to display. If he continues to find it difficult to recognize the words on their own, continue to play games with them in the sentences until you think he will recognize them out of context.

If you have time, try to play the 'Read my sentence' and 'Make a sentence' games described on pages 161 and 162. Remember that learning one or two words a week is good progress and that by doing this, the 36 words you have been asked to teach will take only just over a term to learn.

My daughter loves books and we have read stories to her since she was a baby but the books she is bringing back to read for herself she finds very boring and she wants me to read to her rather than for her to read her books. I do try to sit down with her and hear her read but after two pages she says she is 'dead bored' and gets up to go to play with her baby sister. What should I do?

When children start to read, they are given very simple books – the books may only have two or three words on a page – and children who are used to books telling them exciting stories can feel let down when they are asked to read for themselves. Luckily these first readers are rarely longer than 12 pages.

One way to encourage your child to read the book is to take it in turns to read a page each and then agree that when you have finished the book she can choose a book for you to read to her. Remember to praise her for her reading and to say how pleased you are with her reading.

Another way around this is to play games with the words – let her read the words on one page and then challenge her to find one of the words before you do. You could then switch roles and ask her to tell you a word to find before she does. As she has selected the word she is very likely to win! Do this with several pages or as long as she seems keen to continue.

She might get over the 'boredom factor' if you ask her to read her books to her baby sister. Explain that her sister needs very easy books and let her take the role of the adult and ask her sister to find things in the pictures as well as reading her the words.

As she becomes a better reader she will find that the books from school will get much more interesting and she is likely to start to enjoy reading. However, if she continues to be reluctant to read to you, ask her teacher if there are other books, perhaps from a different scheme, that might suit her better.

My seven-year-old-son is a very good reader and has devoured the reading books sent home from school but now we seem to have run out of books that are suitable for him. He will pick up any book and have a go at reading it but these are often beyond his comprehension. The school says that he has really exhausted their reading books and just send him to the school library to select a book – but the non-fiction books are often too technical and the fiction books are more suitable for older children. What should I do?

The most important thing is to keep your son keen to read so it is important not to let him have books that are beyond his understanding. Look at the books you are reading to him – are they books that he might be able to read on his own with your help? Go to the public library and explain that you have this problem as they will have a much wider selection than the school library and are very knowledgeable about the levels of books and the ones that appeal to the avid reader. If you have a children's bookshop near by, ask for advice there – again they have extensive knowledge of books that are both suitable and popular and your son will not be alone in reading well above his chronological age. He might also enjoy reading books that he has seen on a DVD – these are more likely to be within his comprehension level as when we have seen a film we already have an understanding of the story and we are more confident to tackle the fuller version provided in a book. The sales of classical novels rockets after people have seen a version on the TV! Knowing the story rarely spoils reading the book as having some knowledge about the content allows the reader to search for more information rather than just trying to find out what happens.

My daughter started off quite keen to read but now she is nearly seven years old all she wants to do is to watch the TV or play on her computer when she gets back from school. It is quite difficult to get her to sit still long enough to read her reading book and she is not really keen for me to read to her any longer. I have tried turning the TV off but that always ends in a tantrum which is both exhausting and annoying. What should I do?

When children get back from school they are often quite tired and just want to sit – so being entertained and sitting without having to make much of an effort is very attractive. However, allowing this to extend into all the time between school and bed is not acceptable to any parent. Why not come to an agreement that your daughter can watch TV for approximately 30 minutes when she gets home from school but that after this time the TV/computer will be turned off until you have both finished your work? It is a good idea to share with her what she would most like to see or play so that she chooses the TV or the computer game and she will also know when this comes to an end. Praise her for choosing and also for ending the session.

Set a kitchen timer and show her how long you are going to ask her to read with you (for example, eight minutes to start with) so that she also understands that this is not going to take for ever but that you do expect her to try her best. Praise her and reward her in some way every time she does as you ask. This might be a sticker chart or points or a reward of a more substantial order if you wish. This is a kind of bribery and corruption but it is important that she learns to take control of her time.

My son is nearly six years old and he is not reading as well as his friends. He tells me that he is in the bottom group for reading and that he does not like reading. I try to help him with his reading every night but this is difficult and he always says he does not want to read. I can't understand why he can read a word on one page with no hesitation and then cannot make any attempt to read it on the next page. I have asked the school what to do but they assure me that he will 'take off' one day but that it is just taking a little longer than his friends.

Some children take longer than others to settle into a school routine and this will affect their learning to start with but many of these children do 'catch up' as they become more confident. It is essential to try to support him in his learning and to continue to show him what reading can offer. Try to ensure that you read books to him that he enjoys and that he sees how important it is to you. Obviously you want him to learn to read but if he starts to believe that he cannot do this then it is an uphill job to get him to change his mind.

Helping children with reading is a slow and sometimes painful process but the secret lies in small, regular amounts. Why not show your child a kitchen timer and explain that you will ask him to read to you for just five minutes each day? When the ring sounds, stop and reward him in some way. This could be a chart where you put a sticker on each time he reads to you (not as a judgement as to how well he read but because he did sit down and try). When he has filled the chart perhaps you could reward him with something else. You could draw a simple rocket with five partitions and place a sticker in each section until he reaches the top. What is very important is for him to try to read to you or another adult at least five times a week and that these times are successful and enjoyable. The more anxious you become the more your child will also feel stressed.

Ask his teacher if there are books that he can manage to read at home without too many problems. Start sharing these with him so that he begins to realize that he can read. You could take it in turns to read a page each, or you could start the book and then invite him to read simultaneously with you. At first he is likely to slightly echo your words but as he becomes more confident he will begin to lead this reading and may eventually suggest that he can do it 'on my own.' Remember to tell your son how pleased you are when he reads to you.

Do not worry if he seems to manage a word on one page but forgets it by the next. When you have finished reading the book look back through the pages and ask him to find words on a page that you know he can read. Be really pleased at his success. Then ask him to find the word that he seemed to get intermittently. Finding a problem word is much easier than reading it but as your son looks for it he will be paying attention to how it looks and this will help him to recognize it next time. As his word recognition increases and he sees how pleased you and his teacher are, so his attitude to learning to read will slowly change. Beware of comparing him to his friends, especially voicing your concerns where he might overhear, and try to notice what he can do and be delighted with what he does achieve.

Summary

- Children's reading development does not progress in steady steps. There will be peaks and plateaus. This is perfectly normal. It is important that you support your child when progress in reading is going well *and* when it seems to be at a standstill.
- There are many reading games and activities you can do at home that will support your child's reading development.
- Remember – it is just as important to read to your child as it is to hear your child read.

08

children who can read (7–11 years)

In this chapter you will learn:
- why children who are considered 'good' readers at age 7 can become below average readers at age 11
- how to help your child make good book choices
- how to keep your child reading
- how to support the avid reader.

Medicine for the soul

Inscription over the door of the library at
Thebes (300 BC)

CONGRATULATIONS! With your help (and the efforts of the school) your child has learned to read. Now your child is able to:

- read chapter books with only line drawings
- read silently
- choose books she enjoys (fiction and non-fiction)
- pick up anything and read it (although if she does not find it interesting she quickly puts it down!)
- recall what she has read and talk about characters and themes.

What an achievement!

It is all too easy to believe that your work in supporting your child's reading is over and that now she is sailing solo on the ocean of reading. The danger is that it might not be just you who thinks that there is no longer any need to persevere with reading!

Why might children stop reading?

Your child might think that she can stop reading now she has finished the graded reading scheme of books that previously marked her progress to becoming a reader. This loss of structure can result in a loss of motivation or incentive for reading and once the habit of reading fades it can be very hard to re-ignite. When moving up the levels of the school's hierarchy of books, children have a clear route to reading. Once they reach the top they can feel as though they have no map for the reading journey ahead.

'Free' readers

Some schools describe children who have reached the top of the reading scheme as 'free' readers. This usually means that these children are encouraged to choose freely from books in the school library (or class book corner). Of course, this assumes that children are competent at selecting books at an appropriate level of difficulty and at an interest level that is suitable for their age. However, if children regularly select books that are too hard for them, or books which do not appeal to them, then their enthusiasm for reading can quickly diminish and it is all too easy for these children to become children who can read but don't (see Chapter 10).

Making wise book choices

Many adults will admit that they find it quite difficult to find a book that really appeals. Web-based bookshops acknowledge this by having a pop-up box feature when someone makes a book choice: 'People who bought this book also bought …' It can safely be assumed that they only do this because people have taken advantage of the service and accordingly bought more books.

Children can easily be lost as readers if they do not have a constant supply of books that appeal to them and which are written at a level that gives them a 'comfortable' read.

How do I judge if a book is the right level for my child?

It can be quite difficult to judge the reading level of a book. However, if you are in a bookshop, on the web or in a public library, there are some questions you can ask yourself which will help your child to make good decisions:

- Does the book look the right length? That is, not so short that she will read it in one half-hour session but not so long that it will take her three weeks to plough through.
- Does the blurb on the back sound like the book is targeting children of a similar age to your child?
- Is the author one your child has read (and enjoyed!) before?
- Is the book one of a series? This is often an indication that it is popular, for example, 'Horrid Henry' or 'Harry Potter'.
- If your child is newly fluent then things such as the size of print will make a difference to how she perceives the difficulty of the book. Small print suggests to her that it is more difficult (even if it is not!).
- If your child is with you, ask her to read the first page. Does it appeal?
- Use the 'five finger test'. Turn to the middle of the book. Ask your child to glance down the page and to count off on the fingers of one hand, any words she does not know. If she has used all four fingers (and thumb) before she has got to the

end of the page then the book is going to be a reading challenge. That does not mean she shouldn't try to read it but she should be aware that it will be quite difficult for her to read.

- Is the non-fiction book on a topic your child is interested in? Has it got dramatic photos and page-turning facts?

How to keep your child reading

The number one priority is to continue reading to your child. Although your child is perfectly capable of reading on her own, if you continue to participate in her reading, this will keep her interest in reading alive. She will not want you to always be reading aloud to her (she can read much more quickly to herself), but if you maintain a time when you read aloud to her it can become something really special.

Read books together that are slightly in advance of books your child is reading independently

Tempting your child with more challenging reading can be a real incentive for her to be adventurous in her reading choices. When you read books that have a rich vocabulary and more complex sentence constructions you are providing a model for her of how to read these more sophisticated books. In due course, she will want to read them for herself.

For example, your child may be enjoying the Roald Dahl books, so don't read Roald Dahl to them. Read Philip Ridley, Ian Whybrow or Lemony Snickett. These books are equally fast-paced (and slightly irreverent!) but they represent a small increase in terms of reading challenge.

Children who can read might not want you to read to them every night. Why not make it something for special occasions, for example, on holiday or at weekends?

When you read aloud to your child (even though she can read herself) you are doing more than just allowing her the enjoyment of hearing something read to her. You are demonstrating how good readers read, and you are showing your child that reading is not just for school but that it matters in your home life too.

Provide a plentiful supply of books

Once they have cracked the code of reading, some children really take off and read voraciously. The only thing that will halt this enthusiasm is a lack of books. You therefore need to keep them reading with a constant supply of appealing books. These books do not need to be at your child's reading level – it is perfectly OK to be reading easy books, comics, joke books and magazines (just as an adult reader would).

Make friends with the librarian

To feed your child's reading habit you will need lots of books. However, you do not need to buy all these books, as this is where libraries come in. The children's section of public libraries will have staff who will be skilled at knowing exactly which book will appeal next to your child. Often libraries have 'readathons' (challenges to read so many books over the holidays). Many children like the idea of working towards a certificate and this can inspire their reading further.

Finding the 'next' book

Some children can feel quite bereft when they come to the end of a series of books by a particular author. (Some grandparents may relate to this when they were reading Enid Blyton!) Fortunately, today, there is a wealth of books for children to choose from but they will need guidance to make good choices.

A very useful book is *Who Next ...? A Guide to Children's Authors* (see 'Taking it further', page 235). It provides lists of writers of children's fiction and against each name suggests authors who write in a similar way.

Matching the content of a book with your child's emotional developmental stage

Some children romp ahead with their reading and it can be hard to keep them supplied with books. They may stray into books that are at their reading level but which have themes and content more suitable for the secondary school pupil. One teacher was shocked to find that a seven-year-old was reading a fairly explicit Judy Blume novel about teenage pregnancy. The seven-year-old had no problems with the vocabulary in the book but was perplexed by some of the issues!

(NB For many excellent suggestions about keeping children reading see Chapter 10, page 210.)

Frequently asked questions

Is it possible for a child to read too much?

Some children get so hooked on books that they read to the exclusion of all other hobbies. Like anything taken to excess, this is not healthy. If you suspect your child is reading to avoid doing other things (and not just jobs around the house or having to play with a younger sibling!) then it is worth taking a long hard look at what is going on. Some children read to escape a reality which they may find uncomfortable or unhappy. Investigate to determine if your child's excessive reading is because they feel threatened in social situations. Are they being bullied or excluded?

My son, aged nine, is an average reader. He says all the books at school are boring. What can I do?

Your child is just at the age when children think lots of things at school are 'boring'! Nevertheless, some children can find it difficult to select a 'suitable' book from the school library. Many children still need guidance to make a good choice of books and without that guidance they can sense that nothing appeals.

Your first port of call might be the local library where the librarian will have a fund of ideas about what will appeal to nine-year-old boys. The library might even have a list of books that you could come away with and look up on a website together with your son.

Does he have any particular hobbies? Sometimes that can trigger an interest in reading and the school library might not have many books on, for example, kick boxing!

My daughter is quite a good reader but her social life is so full that she has no time for reading.

Most busy adults do not have much time for reading during the day but they manage to squeeze in 15 minutes' reading at bedtime. Encourage your daughter to do the same. Have a good supply of appealing (and not too difficult) books beside her bed.

I have always enjoyed reading to my son (aged ten) but now he doesn't want me to read to him. Should I insist on reading aloud to him?

There is not much point trying to be too insistent – he will vote with his feet! You could try to tempt him with books that you know he would not read without you, such as longer funny poems or even a play script. See the suggestions for holiday reading in Chapter 10 (page 219) as you might be able to rekindle an interest in reading aloud on holiday.

My daughter, aged 11, loves reading and she is a good reader but she only reads from a very narrow range of fiction. She says she hates non-fiction. Is this OK?

It's great that your daughter has found what she enjoys reading but most of the reading she will be doing in secondary school will be non-fiction. All the text books are non-fiction as are the screen-based texts that will be used in the lessons. If your daughter is so unfamiliar with reading non-fiction she may be surprised when she gets to secondary school to find she is not as good a reader as she thought she was! You could try to tempt her with non-fiction books on topics that really appeal. Does she have any hobbies – dancing, riding or crafts? There are plenty of fun-to-read books on all these topics and it might be a way to get some balance into your daughter's reading diet.

Summary

- Don't stop reading to your child just because she can read for herself.
- Find out what your child likes in a book and make sure there are plenty of those around for her to read.
- Talk to your child about what she is reading. If you can, read what she has read, then you are the best critic and confidant!

09

children who find reading difficult (7–11 years)

In this chapter you will learn:
- reasons why some children find learning to read very difficult
- practical tips to help children who are struggling with reading
- what to do if you think your child is dyslexic
- how to make the best of the partnership between school and home
- how to keep your child enthusiastic about reading.

Me dad can't read and he says it's his fault that I can't and me mam tries to help us but she couldn't read – not till she was a woman – and I'll never be one of them!

Stephen, aged nine, from Tyneside

Why do some children find it more difficult than others to learn to read?

If there was a simple answer to this question then there would not be any children who had difficulties with reading! We would have answers at our fingertips the moment a child showed any difficulties and we would solve all the problems. Unfortunately, the reasons why some children struggle with reading are many and various and it is not easy to diagnose the problem (or to find a solution). The cause of literacy difficulties is one of the most investigated areas of educational research but none of the experts has come up with failsafe answers. This is because learning to read (and write) is a complex process and it can be very difficult identifying why it has gone wrong for a particular child.

How will I know if my child is having literacy difficulties?

This is not so easy to answer as you might think. Learning to read and write is a long slow process and most children do not move along the path at a steady rate. They may have a spurt of progress and then plateau for a while. So it is hard for a parent to identify whether their child is just in one of those plateaus (from which they will naturally emerge in time) or whether the lack of progress is indicative of more serious problems. The best advice if you are worried about your child's progress is to arrange to speak to your child's class teacher.

What if my child is not as good at reading as his best friend?

Of course, the most natural thing is to want to compare your child's performance with his peers but this can be misleading. It is not necessarily the first child to learn to read who goes on to be the most proficient reader. Some children take longer on that initial journey but then have more established skills to sustain them through the later stages of reading development. Like many other skills children acquire, there is no guaranteed age at which each aspect of the skill is achieved.

The potty training analogy

It can be quite helpful to compare learning to read with potty training. Some toddlers have the control (and inclination) to be 'dry' (day and night) by the age of two. Others are three before they have achieved this skill and others may be nearer to four before they can manage without a nappy at night. Does this mean that the first children to abandon nappies will be the most reliable at getting to the loo on time or that because they were relatively quick at achieving this social skill they are necessarily 'better' at using the toilet for the rest of their lives? The truth of the matter is that the fact that your child is slower than his best friend to grasp the purpose of the potty is of great significance to you *at the time when the best friend has the skill and your child doesn't!* Once your child has also acquired the control to get to the potty on time then you quickly forget that there was any time difference in the acquisition of that skill in the first place. (The same goes for crawling, learning to walk, etc.)

Don't panic!

What the potty analogy demonstrates is that children acquire all sorts of skills at different rates. Some may make impressive strides with reading and then seem to be stuck at a particular stage. Others may not seem to get the hang of the skill in the first place and then suddenly it all clicks into place. These stops and starts are all entirely natural and should not send parents into panic.

One thing is pretty certain about acquiring the skills of reading: if parental pressure is excessive this will have a deleterious effect upon the child's progress. This is particularly true if your child has hit a plateau in his learning. It is natural to be concerned and to want the very best for your child but this desire should not create an air of anxiety about learning to read as this will definitely hinder his progress.

Keep 'reading at home' sessions stress-free

If you sense your child is not making satisfactory progress along the long road to becoming a reader then your number one priority should be to ensure that all shared reading sessions at home are as enjoyable and stress-free (and frequent) as you can possibly manage. Just because your child is having what might be a slight blip in his journey to successful, independent reading is not a reason for cutting down on the amount of fun reading sessions you have together. If you reduce the times you read to your child in order to have more opportunities to hear him read you may well be denying him the only really interesting and enjoyable experience he has of reading. Restricting the number of times you read to him might also be removing any incentive for him to persevere with the skills of reading. So the more difficulties your child experiences in learning to read, the more you should spend time at home reading to your child, talking about books and generally making time with books as pleasurable as possible.

Why might my child be having difficulties with reading?

The reason your child may be finding it hard to make progress with reading might be because he is missing one of the ingredients of reading skills. These skills include:

- the ability to map speech sounds on to the letters of the alphabet (phonics) (see page 143)
- being able to recognize familiar words quickly (word recognition) (page 144)
- understanding that the printed word makes sense and that it is communicating with the reader (comprehension).

(**NB** See Chapter 07 for further details on the elements of the reading process.)

Difficulties with phonics

Some children's difficulties are associated with the phonic aspects of reading. These difficulties can arise for a number of reasons:

- They may not be able to hear clearly the fine distinctions between the sounds of the different letters (for example, the difference between the sound 'b' and 'p').
- They may find it extremely hard to remember what sound a letter (or combination of letters) makes.
- They may be able to hear the individual sounds but have not realized that they should be blending those sounds when trying to read an unfamiliar word.

Clarity of hearing

As outlined in Chapter 07, the skill of mapping phonemes (sounds) on to graphemes (letters) and then blending the phonemes smoothly to read a word is dependent upon sophisticated auditory discrimination. Some children may lack the ability to make those distinctions because of 'glue ear'.

What is glue ear?

Glue ear is a condition which causes fluid to build up in the middle ear. Where there should be air in the Eustachian tube there is fluid. This condition is very common. More than seven in ten children have at least one episode of glue ear before they are four years old. In most cases it only lasts a short while. Boys are more commonly affected than girls and it is most common in children who:

- live in homes where people smoke
- were bottle-fed rather than breast-fed
- have frequent colds or chest infections
- have a brother or sister who had glue ear.

Generally glue ear occurs after the child has had a cold. It results in some loss of hearing. This hearing loss may not be obvious in ordinary day-to-day living but when it comes to hearing the minute differences between sounds, then any hearing impairment can affect the child's ability in this aspect of reading.

Did you know?

Over the telephone the letters 'b' and 'p', 's' and 'f', and 'm' and 'n' can easily be confused. Because of this confusion, a system of internationally recognized radio call signs – the NATO (North Atlantic Treaty Organization) phonetic alphabet – was created. The alphabet assigns a word to illustrate the name of each letter:

A = Alpha
B = Bravo
C = Charlie
D = Delta
E = Echo
etc.

The purpose of this alphabet was to avoid potential confusion between letters in circumstances when accuracy is crucial, for example, radio calls from aircraft to the control tower or police calls to the police station; or even when giving your postcode over the phone to a supplier. So a postcode SN4 1BM (which could be misheard as FM4 1PN) could be clearly conveyed as **S**ierra **N**ovember 4 1 **B**ravo **M**ike.

Hearing the letter names and hearing the letter sounds

The fact that a phonetic alphabet needed to be created underlines the difficulty of hearing individual letters. But the letter names used in the NATO phonetic alphabet – A B C D etc. – although potentially confusing, are still much more distinctive than the *sounds* each letter makes, which is what children are expected to recognize as they learn phonics. Hearing the difference between the sound 'b' and the sound 'p' or between the short vowel sound 'a' and the short vowel sound 'e' requires very accurate hearing indeed and any child with any incidences of minor hearing loss (such as glue ear) would be severely disadvantaged.

How does glue ear affect children's success with reading?

What sometimes happens is that a child has intermittent hearing loss (due to a heavy cold or glue ear) and they miss out on some crucial teaching of the association of sounds to some letters.

They simply cannot hear the difference between some sounds and they do not understand what the teacher is expecting them to do. When the cold is over and their hearing is more accurate some children pick up on the elements they missed out on and no long-term damage is done to their progress in reading.

However, other children may have become so muddled by their lack of ability to distinguish the sounds that they abandon any attempt to use phonics as a means of decoding words. They have tried it as a strategy but because of their inaccurate hearing it has not been a successful strategy, so they give up on it entirely. These children will need a re-introduction into the relationship between sounds and letters in the English language which (as Chapter 07 outlines) is a very complicated relationship.

Keep a balanced approach

Although you (and your child's school) may have identified that the reason for your child's lack of progress in reading might be attributed to his poor understanding of how sounds map on to letters, this does not mean that you should abandon all other reading experiences with your child in order to concentrate on this missing component. Remembering which letters make which sounds is, in many respects, the most boring part of reading! It is certainly the most mechanical aspect of the skill and the most 'ephemeral', in that, from the child's point of view, it has little or nothing to do with the aspects of reading and books that most appeal to children, that is, enjoying funny or scary stories or discovering amazing facts in an information book. So while you will want to support the school as they introduce a remediation programme to help your child pick up on the aspects of phonics he missed earlier (when affected by minor hearing loss) your best strategy is to link this knowledge to the reading that you share together with your child on a regular basis. So don't put away all the fun books and buy a 'scheme' which promises to teach your child phonics, as all you will be teaching him is that reading isn't the fun thing he thought it was! But you can help him to make the important association between letters and sounds *as you read to him*.

Activities to support learning phonics

The best way to help your child tune in to the sounds in words is to play games with words as you read to him. When you have read a story or information book to your child, choose a page and challenge your child to:

- find a word starting with the sound …
- find a word ending with the sound …
- find two words which start with the same sound
- find the word that is made by blending these sounds (then sound out a word, for example, w/e/n/t).

NB You must sound out the letters according to the sound they make in the word, so the 'ou' letters in 'out' would be sounded 'ow' (as in the word h/ow), but in the word 'soup' the 'ou' letters are sounded 'oo'. See Chapter 07, page 144 for more information on the sounds the letters make.

Top tip

Don't let these phonic challenges become a bore to your child. Keep the games fun and if your child can't answer any questions, tell him the answer and move on. Do not draw attention to his failure.

Another top tip!

Sometimes children (especially boys) respond better to a challenge when you imply that they won't be able to meet your challenge. So you might like to say things like:

'I bet you can't find two words that begin with the phoneme …'
'I bet I can find a word that has the sound … in the middle quicker than you can.'

(Of course, you must discreetly allow your child to just find the answer before you do!)

I spy

'I spy' is a good way to draw attention to the sounds in words. You can 'spy' an object with a particular sound at the beginning, in the middle or at the end of a word. For example:

I spy with my little eye something that begins with the sound 't' (television).

I spy with my little eye something that ends with the sound 'o' (video).

I spy with my little eye something that has the 'A' sound in the middle (table).

Get it wrong!

When you are reading to your child (ideally from a familiar story or information book) make a deliberate mistake. So, for example, instead of reading:

'Little Red Riding Hood skipped along the <u>path</u> through the wood.'

say:

'Little Red Riding Hood skipped along the <u>bath</u> through the wood.'

Your child will quickly hear that something has gone wrong. At first you could feign ignorance saying 'What? What's the matter?' This forces your child to put into words what you have done wrong. So he might say, 'You said "bath" instead of "path".' Then you have two possible courses of action:

1 You could either get him to find the word on the page and to double check that it is 'path' and it starts with a 'p'.
2 You could say, 'You're right! I said "bath" when I should have said "path". Which part of the word did I get wrong? What do I have to change to put it right?'

NB If you make your mistakes as silly as possible this not only increases the fun your child will have in identifying the mistake (and putting it right) but he will also listen all the more intently for your next slip-up. Children find it funniest if the 'wrong' word is a little bit rude so saying 'bum' instead of 'mum' will increase their enjoyment in the game!

Top tip

Only play this game after you have shared the book with your child without making any mistakes. Make your 'mistakes' in the following way:

- Choose a word which rhymes with the correct word, so read 'hair' instead of 'bear'. For example, 'In the dark cave was a big (leave a dramatic pause) hair.' This draws attention to the sound at the beginning of the word.
- Choose a word which starts the same way as the correct word. For example, 'In the dark' (leave a dramatic pause) and then start the word 'ca...' but say 'cage' (instead of 'cave') was a big bear.'

Robot reading

Warn your child that you are going to read some words 'like a robot'. This means you are going to separate out the sounds in the word. The challenge for your child is to blend the sounds to make the word before you move on to read the next word. So you might read:

'In the d-ar-k' (child quickly says 'dark' and you continue reading as if there had been no interruption) 'cave there was a big bear.'

> **Top tip**
>
> Do not stop too frequently to draw attention to the phonic features of words. If your child senses you have over-stepped the boundary between 'fun reading' and 'serious work' he may not be so co-operative!

More challenging phonic activities

If your child can do all of the above activities successfully it is time to move on to the next level of challenge.

Even at this higher level, the best way to help your child to make the crucial connections between sounds and letters is by not drawing attention to these skills in isolation. Help your child to see how knowing his sounds relates to the skill of reading.

Using the technique mentioned earlier of 'I bet you can't ...' draw attention to the letter (or, sometimes, letters) which make the sound. So, for example, when reading the sentence: 'Percy could see the carriage in the siding' say to your child: 'Can you find two words with the sound "ee"?' ('Percy' and 'see'). If necessary, repeat these words with a slight emphasis on the shared 'ee' sound: 'Percy', 'see'. Then ask your child to look at the words in turn. 'What is making the "ee" sound in "Percy"?' (the letter 'y') 'What is making the "ee" sound in "see"?' (the letters 'ee').

Top tip

If your child is enjoying these word detective games, you could suggest that you keep a list of all the words that have a particular sound in a special book. Choose one of the 'long vowel sounds' as these have the greatest range of different letters that make the same sound. So, for example, select the sound 'A' and every time either of you notices a word that has the 'A' sound jot it down on a page with columns to represent the particular sound. So you might have a page with the following completed columns:

a-e	ay	a	ea
make	play	station	great
same	day	acorn	

(See Appendix 1, page 223 for examples of long vowel phonemes.)

Talk to your child's teacher

It is a really good idea to find out how your child's teacher is helping him to make up on lost ground in his phonic knowledge. Try to understand what the school is trying to do so you can give them maximum support at home. However, this does not mean that you need to do exactly the same activities that your child is doing in school. This could make the whole learning to read business very dull for your child. What you do at home should be complementary to the skills your child is being taught in school.

If you feel you might be muddling your child because you are unsure how to do some of the phonic activities, such as sounding out words, then ask the school if they have a coaching CD that could help you to practise the skills of identifying sounds in words and then blending those sounds to read the words. You can then practise in the comfort of your own home with a simple game on the CD. Some government produced resources have training CDs for teaching assistants and these can be a very helpful way for parents to gain confidence that they are supporting their child's phonic development appropriately.

Warning signs

If you feel that despite your best efforts to help your child identify individual sounds in words, he seems unable to do so, it might be worth arranging for him to have a hearing test. It is most unlikely that any serious hearing loss would not have been picked up at a health visitor check-up but any minor impairment could go a long way to explain why your child finds the phonic element of reading so difficult to acquire and it may be that you should concentrate your energies at home on the aspects of reading your child finds more manageable. For example, he may be growing in confidence in his ability to quickly recognize words on sight, or he may be getting better and better at remembering what you have read together and he may be able to answer quite detailed questions about what happens in a story. These are really valuable elements in the reading process and playing to your child's strengths may make the sessions at home stress-free and fun while allowing the experts in school to tackle the aspects of reading your child is finding a challenge.

Case study: Liam aged nearly seven

Liam's birthday is in August and he is one of the youngest pupils in his Y2 class (ages 6–7). At home his parents do spend time reading with him but time is short as Liam's four-year-old brother is very demanding.

When Liam started school he seemed to be progressing with reading as well as any of his peers, but as the end of Y2 approaches, the teacher assessments of Liam's progress have identified that his reading ability is below average.

When Liam was four he had a spate of colds and ear infections which meant that his hearing acuity at the start of school was less than 100 per cent.

Liam used to love book sharing sessions with his parents (particularly his dad) but his parents have noticed that in the last six months Liam has seemed less relaxed in the times when they read to him and he prefers to be playing on the computer or watching TV instead of sharing books before bedtime.

Liam's school uses a lively, interactive programme for teaching phonics and for these sessions the children are grouped according to their competence in phonic knowledge. Recently

Liam has become one of only three Y2 children still in a phonics group with Y1 pupils. Liam has been saying for some time that he doesn't like doing phonics and he thinks it is 'silly'. The school has increased the number of phonic lessons Liam has, in order to give him one final 'push' before he goes up to the Juniors (Y3).

Liam's mum and dad sensed that his reading development was at a standstill but they didn't know what to do. They decided to arrange a meeting with Liam's class teacher where they could all discuss how Liam could be helped. The teacher gave up 30 minutes after school one day and Liam's mum and dad were able to get away from work early to talk through the options. The teacher showed them that Liam could:

- recognize 40 simple words on sight
- recall a story if it was read to him
- give a sound to 30 out of the 44 sounds in the English language (i.e. he was able to look at the letter 'g' and give the sound /g/ but he was not able to give a sound to the letters 'gh' in the word 'laugh'. He was generally applying 'one letter = one sound.' This meant he would sound out 'cat' as c/a/t but he would also sound out 'laugh' as l/a/u/g/h (instead of l/au/gh).

The teacher explained that the school were concentrating on teaching Liam the remaining 14 sounds (these were all 'long vowel sounds' such as 'ou', 'ea', 'ie' or some of the consonant digraphs such as 'sh', 'ch' or 'gh').

The school had also identified that although Liam could give a sound to many of the letters in the alphabet, he had not confidently grasped the skill of *blending* the sounds to read the words. For example, he was finding it difficult to smoothly blend 't' on to 'r' to read the word 'trap'.

Liam's parents and his teacher came up with a plan of action. For the remaining two months of infant school and for the two months of the summer holiday before Liam started in the junior school, they would have clear roles to work in a co-ordinated way to help Liam.

The school would persevere with teaching Liam the sounds he could not yet recognize but these would be presented to Liam on a chart where all the sounds he could already recognize were marked with a gold star. Them Liam was invited to choose one of the 'missing' sounds and to make that his next focus to learn. His goal was to be able to recognize that sound (to hear it, see it, say it and write it) and then he could have a gold star next to that sound. Every time a new gold star was added to Liam's chart he would have a reward, for example, a word of praise in the 'hall of fame' at an assembly, five more minutes of 'golden time', a point for his house team or a sticker, etc.

Liam's parents were asked to help Liam with the blending aspect of phonic knowledge – that is the skill of running the sounds of a word together quickly so that Liam could recognize what word was made up of those smoothly blended sounds. Liam's parents built this in to their reading together sessions at home. They made a real effort to read with Liam every night. They took it in turns so that one of them read to Liam's brother and the other concentrated on Liam.

A typical bedtime reading session went like this:

Liam's dad would listen to Liam read from the book the school sent home for reading practice. He would look for opportunities to praise Liam, for example, if he read a line correctly; if he said any of the words with appropriate expression; if he went back and corrected a word he had initially got wrong. Liam's dad did not ask him to 'sound out' any word that Liam could not immediately recognize. He gave Liam five seconds to try to work out the word but if he couldn't do so after that time, he would say each sound in the word and challenge Liam to blend the sounds to make the word. Then he encouraged Liam to say the word and then continue with the reading.

When Liam had finished reading his school book, Liam's dad would choose Liam's favourite book of the moment and read that to him. During the reading, Liam's dad would occasionally stop and play some of the phonic games described on pages 186–7 ('Get it wrong', 'Robot reading' and 'More challenging phonic activitics'). Liam's dad tried to keep everything as a game and gave Liam lots of praise.

By the end of term, Liam was secure with 42 of the 44 speech sounds and he told his mum he thought phonics was fun!

Difficulties with word recognition

Some children's difficulties are associated with the whole word recognition aspect of reading. These difficulties can arise for a number of reasons:

- Children may not realize that good readers make an effort to remember words that occur frequently. (We call these words the 'high frequency words' – see Appendix 1 and Chapter 07 for more information.)
- Children may have become dependent upon phonics and think they must sound out each word before saying it. This may be because they lack the confidence to say a word outright or it may be that they use the sounding out process to buy them time to work out what the word might be.
- Children may find it difficult to remember words out of context.

Clarity of vision

The ability to recognize high frequency words quickly is dependent upon:

- accurate vision to identify each letter shape swiftly
- an understanding of how sounds map on to those letter shapes
- storing the patterns of those associated sounds and letter shapes, firstly in the visual memory and ultimately in the lexical memory (this is the part of the brain where whole words and their meanings are stored).

Some children may be slow to acquire the skills of instant word recognition because their eyesight is insufficiently accurate. Learning to read requires visual acuity in excess of any demands previously placed upon the child, so any very minor eyesight inaccuracies may not be detected until a child is expected to observe the minute differences in appearance between, for example, n and h.

Test of eyesight

Before you rush your child off to the optician you could test his eyesight with a simple game at home:

1 Cut up a piece of card in 2 cm squares making 20 squares in total.

2 In the centre of each card write one of the following letters in lower case letters, no bigger than 3 mm: b d f g h i j n t y. The reason the letters need to be small is because you are trying to replicate the size of print children see in early reading books in the classroom. (These letters have been chosen because they are similar in appearance.)

3 Write the same letters (in as similar a style as you can) on the remaining ten squares.

4 Tell your child you are going to play 'Letter pairs'. Turn all 20 cards face down and spread them out on a table. Challenge your child to turn over two cards and to say whether the cards are a pair (i.e. the same letter). If they are, your child can keep them as a pair. If not, he must return the cards face down on the table back in the spaces they were originally.

5 Then he continues trying to find matching pairs.

Your role is to see how easy it is for him to do the checking process. So, for the purposes of this assessment, it is not so much his ability to remember where a letter is on the table, but to judge how swiftly he can determine if the letters he has picked are the same. If your child has to spend more than two seconds determining if, for example, 'i' and 'j' are the same, then it might be worth taking him to an optician for a more accurate eye test.

If your child can determine in two seconds or less that the two cards match (or don't match) then it is very unlikely that your child's difficulty stems from visual impairment.

NB If your child is quick at judging whether the two cards he has turned over are a match, but he is slow at remembering where each letter is on the table, then his difficulties are more to do with general memory training and it is a good idea to play lots of games at home that train the memory. These games do not need to focus on matching letters or words, they could be matching pictures or patterns.

> **Top tip**
>
> Playing these sorts of games on the computer can be more fun than just playing with cards.

Helping children improve at word recognition

If you feel confident that your child does not have any eyesight problems that are affecting his ability to see whole words and you have played memory games to help him to improve his memory then the next avenue to pursue is to help him to recognize on sight the first 100 high frequency words.

As explained in Chapter 07, once children have a core of useful words which they can instantly recognize, this frees up their brains to concentrate on decoding (blending the sounds in words to read them). For example, by the age of seven, most children should be able to instantly recognize all the high frequency (HF) words in the following sentence and only need to stop and 'sound out' the less familiar word, 'yard'.

HF HF HF HF HF HF HF HF sound out: y/ar/d

I   can see a   big dog in   the yard

Some children need extra help to remember these words so it is worth discussing with your child's teacher which words he or she thinks your child is still uncertain about.

NB It is sometimes worth starting again with teaching the 'easiest' (or most frequently used) words (see Appendix 2, page 225). The advantage of starting right at the beginning is that your child will undoubtedly have success with some of these words and it is always better to start where a child can feel they are successful as this boosts confidence, rather than starting where the difficulty lies (which can deflate confidence).

Teach words in the context of a sentence

Armed with a list of approximately 25 words create four or five sentences which include these words. As was outlined in Chapter 06, when we teach a child to recognize a word it is important that they learn it first in the context of a sentence, as this gives the word a meaning. It is easy for children to understand the meaning of most nouns (naming words) as they can picture what they might be (dog, television, computer). But they cannot picture 'of', 'so' or 'be'. So we should teach these words in the context of a sentence so that the words have a purpose.

A typical sentence might be: 'The cat was by the door.' (See Appendix 4, page 227 for examples of other sentences.) In this sentence the high frequency words are 'the', 'was' and 'by'. You could help your child by giving him little pictures next to the nouns ('cat' and 'door').

Write the sentence 'The cat was by the door' on a strip of card. On separate pieces of card write each of the high frequency words: 'The', 'was', 'by' and 'the'. Now:

1 Read the sentence to your child.
2 Ask your child to read the sentence with you.
3 Point at each word in turn and ask your child to say it.
4 Point at each word in a random order and ask your child to say it quickly.
5 Give your child the word cards and ask him to match the words with the corresponding words in the sentence.
6 Shuffle the word cards and give them to your child. See if he can identify each word.

NB Ten minutes is quite enough time to spend on a game like this.

Top tip: Key words on a key ring

Work on one sentence per session and aim to do four ten-minute sessions per week. At the start of a new session, 'test' how well your child can remember the high frequency words from the previous sentence. If he can recognize the word instantly, punch a hole in the corner of the word card and put the card on a key ring. As you work through the sessions you can test the 'key ring' words before you start playing the game. In this way, your child is slowly but steadily building up a bank of words that he can recognize instantly.

Word games as well as reading

Don't forget: word teaching sessions (such as those above) should happen *as well as* times when you read to your child. If you swap all the enjoyable 'read to' sessions with 'word testing' sessions, your child might be put off the idea of books altogether. Embed the word games into a shared reading session. After you have enjoyed a book together is the best time to look back through the book and play 'spot the word'. Choose one of the high frequency words your child has been learning to recognize on sight and challenge your child to find it on the page. Do the same with five different words but no more! You do not want to detract from the pleasure of the book you have just shared together.

Case study: Leanne aged nearly nine

Leanne used to love school and sharing books at home but recently she has shown signs of anxiety about reading. When she reads to her mum at home she slowly sounds out every word. She is usually able to blend the sounds accurately and say the whole word when she has done that, but each word takes her between one and two seconds to read and reading at this slow place often means she loses the flow of what the sentence is all about. Leanne's teacher is pleased with her phonic skills but is keen to enlist help from Leanne's mum to improve Leanne's confidence to look at a word and instantly say what it is.

Leanne and her mum played the sentence and word games outlined on pages 194–6. They built up a key ring of words that Leanne knew she knew. Within a month, Leanne could recognize 100 words on sight. This speeded up her rate of reading and meant that Leanne's understanding of the text also improved. Leanne's enthusiasm for reading has returned and she is now confident using both reading strategies: instant word recognition and accurate phonic blending.

What is dyslexia?

The British Dyslexia Association defines dyslexia as 'a weakness in the processing of language-based information.' Recent investigations using brain imaging techniques have been able to identify which parts of the brain are activated during the process of reading. All the research has been based on adults who have shown serious difficulties in learning to read. The results indicate that some people's brains are less 'hard-wired' for reading than others. These people could be described as dyslexic. It is important to note that dyslexia is not related to IQ (intelligence quotient). This means that someone who has difficulties with sequencing (putting things into a logical sequential order or remembering things in sequential order), short-term memory, organization, spelling and writing might be highly adept in skills that do not require those competencies, for example, mental arithmetic, spatial awareness, extensive spoken vocabulary.

In the world of education there has long been a debate about the existence of dyslexia. The debate revolves around whether dyslexia is a specific condition or an extreme form of general difficulty in learning the skills of reading and writing.

As a very general rule of thumb, if a child has some of the following characteristics then the term dyslexic *might* apply to them:

- average or above average verbal language and reasoning skills
- average or above average mathematical skills
- extreme difficulty in recalling the sound patterns in language
- severe weaknesses in short-term verbal memory
- spelling that is 'bizarre', for example, many children might misspell the word 'went' as 'whent' but the dyslexic might spell it 'tw'.

The dyslexia label

In some respects whether your child has the label 'dyslexic' or whether there are other reasons to explain his literacy difficulties is less important than finding ways to help him. The ways in which your child may be helped to improve will not differ greatly whether he is dyslexic or has other problems with reading. So what matters is to concentrate on how to help children who find reading (and writing) very difficult. Sometimes having a name for a problem can be reassuring. Just as when you go to the doctor feeling really miserable with an extremely sore throat, it can almost give status to our suffering to be told that we have a streptococcal infection of the larynx. We still need to take plenty of fluids and a general analgesic whether it is a common or garden sore throat or something with a fancier name!

It is important for parents to accept if their child is two years or more behind the average of the class in reading and writing that:

- it is not the child's fault
- it is not their fault
- it is most unlikely to be the school's fault.

What matters is not looking around to lay blame somewhere but concentrating on giving as much support to your child as possible. That support might include raising your child's self-esteem as well as embarking on a literacy remediation programme.

The important thing to do is to identify serious difficulties with reading as early as possible. Experts would say that this identification could take place with children as young as six years, four months. If the extent of reading difficulty is not identified early on then children who have a wide discrepancy between their verbal skills and their reading and writing skills can become very frustrated. They see themselves as 'thick' and their self-esteem can plummet. These children can go on to be teenagers who avoid school altogether.

The British Dyslexia Association

The British Dyslexia Association is an organization set up to support children with severe reading difficulties. For a fee they will assess your child and conclude whether, in their opinion, your child is dyslexic.

A certificate of 'dyslexia' may mean you can encourage the school to speed up a meeting with an educational psychologist. Dyslexics are also entitled to extra support in formal examinations – in GCSE examinations in Year 11 and A1 and A2 level examinations in Years 12 and 13. Sometimes technical support in the form of a laptop and voice recognition software is available should your child choose to go to university. For further information see: www.bdadyslexia.org.uk

The educational psychologist

If you are really concerned about the difficulties your child is having with reading you might ask your child's school to arrange for him to have an assessment by the educational psychologist. This expert will run a number of tests and come up with results that will identify precisely the nature of the difficulties your child is experiencing. He or she will suggest a remediation programme to support your child's learning. This may result in your child being allocated specific support from an adult (generally a teaching assistant) on a one-to-one basis. The local authority funding for this support might be between one and two hours a week up to 15 hours a week depending on the severity of the need. It can be quite difficult to set in motion an assessment of your child by an educational psychologist but if you are concerned, and the school shares that concern, then you should persist.

Supporting children who find reading difficult

Although the label 'dyslexic' may not be the most important issue, finding out exactly where your child's difficulties lie is crucial (and the British Dyslexia Association may go some way in outlining this). You should make an appointment with your child's teacher and possibly with the special needs teacher (or inclusion manager) who has specific responsibility for children with literacy difficulties. You should go to this meeting armed with evidence of what your child *can* do, for example, remember the names of even the most obscure dinosaurs, play sophisticated computer games and be a good team member of a football team. All of these things are learned skills which show that your child *can* learn. What he might not be able to do so far, is to master the specific skills required in reading.

You should ask the special needs teacher which specific aspects of reading your child is finding difficult. Is it:

• remembering which letter is which?
• blending sounds smoothly to read a word?
• recognizing a whole word on sight?
• recalling what he has read?

Then you and the school should come up with a plan of action which clearly defines what the school will do and what you will do at home.

Dyslexia – a parents' perspective

My husband and I became aware of the extent of our daughter's difficulties with reading when, aged eight, she could not read 'Park Road' on a road sign. We had, of course, known that Grace found reading difficult and that she was frustrated by her lack of success but it was this small incident that was a wake up call. We then started looking more closely at what Grace could (and couldn't) do. We had both noticed that Grace could sometimes read a word on one page and then get it wrong every other time it occurred in the book. It did make us wonder if she was really trying her best!

Like lots of 'keen' parents we thought we had given Grace an excellent start to her school life. We had always read to her and she enjoyed story times together. When she started bringing reading books home from school we helped her to read them. With the benefit of hindsight, we now think that any success Grace had with those early reading books came about because she was able to make very accurate predictions about what the words were, based on what was going on in the pictures. She also relied on remembering words in the book as the teaching assistant had read it to her during the school day.

Attending parents' evenings at Grace's school

We attended every parents' evening to be told that Grace was 'settling in well', was 'very polite' and 'a popular little girl'. While it was lovely to hear these compliments about our daughter I now realize that we were avoiding the real question: 'How is Grace getting on with reading and writing?'

Grace is an only child, so we had no expectation of what she should be able to do at any particular age. Because the school did not seem to be concerned, neither were we. Looking back, I wish I had asked the teacher directly, 'How is Grace doing compared to her peers?' I know that comparisons can sometimes be unfair but I do believe that parents need some sort of baseline to judge their child's development. Now that I have read a lot more about the subject I know that the Department for Children, Schools and Families in the UK has a Code of Practice for children with special educational needs which says that the guiding principles for professionals should be identifying children whose progress is significantly behind that made by their peers.

Were we just 'pushy' parents?

We made an appointment to speak to Grace's class teacher and the special educational needs teacher. While they were prepared to admit that Grace had some difficulties, they seemed to think that these problems would sort themselves out without any further intervention. They did not suggest that Grace needed extra help in the classroom or that she would need easier books to read. This made us feel like 'pushy' parents – as if we were making a fuss about nothing.

We found a private tutor

We took Grace to a private reading tutor for an assessment. She confirmed our worst fears – that Grace was at least two years behind the expected standard in reading and writing for her age. Grace had weekly tuition with the private tutor and she began to make some progress, although this sometimes felt like one step forward and two steps back. One of the great benefits of taking Grace to a tutor was that the tutor gave us lots of ideas of how to support Grace's learning at home. (See 'Phonic games' on page 157 and 'Sight word games' on page 160.) Grace really enjoyed these one-to-one sessions which she described as 'fun'.

Meeting an educational psychologist

We asked the school to make an appointment with the local authority educational psychologist to assess Grace's needs. We waited a whole year before this meeting actually took place. The educational psychologist's report confirmed that Grace was seriously under-performing for her age. Then, at last, the local authority awarded Grace a statement of special educational needs. This meant that Grace was entitled to one-to-one tuition in school for 12 hours a week.

Grace's British Dyslexia Association assessment

While we were waiting for the local authority to respond, we decided to approach the British Dyslexia Association to ask them to assess Grace. This was quite an expensive business but we felt we had to do something to have professional evidence of Grace's needs.

The British Dyslexia Association confirmed that Grace was dyslexic. We took the report from the British Dyslexia Association to the school and, whether it was coincidental or not, the appointment with the educational psychologist followed shortly after.

Why did Grace 'slip through the net'?

Grace is now nearly ten years of age. She is the happy, confident girl she always was and she is making slow but steady progress with literacy. We recognize that she might always have difficulties in this area but, as parents, we feel we should have intervened earlier to get her the help she needed. We relied on the professionals in the school system to alert us to any problems our daughter had. They were obviously reluctant to label Grace as having learning difficulties because they felt that she would eventually make progress without any extra intervention. They were not uncaring, but because Grace is such an amenable child, they found it difficult to equate her difficulties with those of some boys in the class who were very disruptive and took up a lot of the class teacher's time. Grace is as competent a talker as any child in the class and this might have distracted her teachers from realizing the extent of her reading and writing difficulties. It must also be said that we partly blame ourselves for being so nervous of being labelled 'neurotic' or 'time-wasters' that we held back against our better judgement.

Getting the balance right

In the vast majority of cases, schools are successfully addressing gaps in children's skills for reading. The best strategy to support your child's literacy development at home might be to do as many fun things with books as you can possibly manage. After all, the older your child is, the more aware he will be of his slow rate of progress compared with his peers. A child who stops believing that they can become a reader is a child who is very difficult to help. One of the key roles of a supportive home is to convince your child that you know he is trying his best and to celebrate the things he is good at. Severe dyslexics may have difficulties with reading all their lives but those who emerge out of the school system with their self-esteem intact will almost certainly go on to find employment which allows them to use the skills they have and not be held back by their problems with literacy.

Frequently asked questions

My son, Jayden, is ten. He found reading difficult from the start but he was always prepared to let me help him. Recently he has been very reluctant to let me hear him read. He says he hasn't brought a book home or if he has he finds all sorts of excuses not to read it to me. I know he needs help. Why won't he let me help him?

Your situation is not uncommon. Jayden is probably embarrassed by his poor reading skills and when he gets home he wants nothing more to do with books and reading! You have to accept that he finds reading to you uncomfortable. He may feel it is just confirming what he already thinks – that he is no good at reading. Find some reading matter on a topic that does interest him – a fanzine magazine for a football team, the latest news about a group, a cheat for a hidden level of a computer game. Offer to read these to him with no requirement for him to do any of the reading. Use the sessions to ask him more about his hobby and take an interest so that your questions are worth his while to answer. Occasionally draw attention to words on the page, for example, a word written in capitals or the name of a player that you can't pronounce. Don't be heavy-handed. If he thinks you are trying to trick him into reading to you, he will vote with his feet! Do talk to Jayden's teacher to explain that he is not enjoying reading to you at home. She needs to be aware that he is not getting any extra practice in reading at home. She might suggest that you play some reading or spelling games – either pencil and paper games or computer games which Jayden might find more fun.

There is no point in forcing Jayden to read to you. It will not help his reading development if he hates every minute of it. Try reading together some funny poems. These are often short and so Jayden might not feel daunted by them. Search the library (or Internet) for information books on topics that might tempt him. Be prepared to do the reading but always give him the space to pick up the book later on, if only to browse at the pictures. Alternatively, back off from books and try challenging him with reading and spelling games (with rewards!). For example, take a bet that he can't learn to recognize (and spell) five words from a Key Word list (ask his teacher for suggestions and choose words that you are confident he can acquire without too much effort). Offer to help Jayden with the learning and then when he says he is ready – test him. If he is successful he gets the reward. If not, he has more time to get it right before you test him again.

Alex is nearly eight. He reads to me most evenings but it is a very painful process. He gets slower and slower and quieter and quieter. He obviously hates doing it and I don't know if I should make him do it any more.

Why don't you get a few joke books – particularly those jokes that are based around a question and an answer, for example, 'What goes ha ha bonk?' 'A man laughing his head off.' You should read both the question and answer to Alex but he might be interested in trying to get to the punch line before you so he might be prepared to try to read the 'answer'. Keep the sessions light and fun. Encourage Alex to re-read two of the jokes so that he can remember them to tell his dad later or his granddad at the weekend.

My daughter, Suzi, is nine and a bit. She would love to be able to read the longer chapter books that her friends seem to read so easily. She is getting discouraged. What can I do?

It is important that in school Suzi reads books at her correct reading level. But if she is a bit bored with the easier books that are at her reading level (or she thinks they are a bit babyish) then there is no reason why you shouldn't offer to read to her the books she wishes she could read independently. Don't make these 'reading to' sessions a sneaky way of getting her to do more reading! Accept the fact that you will need to be more hands-on at this stage of Suzi's reading development. Also, whenever you can, buy Suzi CDs of her favourite books so that she can listen to them on her own. Suggest she follows the text with a copy of the book but if she doesn't want to, don't insist.

Alternatively you might decide to 'share' the reading of one of the books. You could do some of the reading and then invite her to read a page before you continue with the reading. In this way Suzi will be able to enjoy the books she wants to read and she will also have had some practice in reading to you. She may find she reads better than usual when she joins in after your reading as she will be concentrating on the meaning of what she is reading and this will help her to recognize the words. One of your priorities at home is that Suzi keeps on enjoying stories, whether she has read them independently or not.

Declan is seven and has just gone up to the junior school. As far as I can tell he is the only one still on his reading level in his class. Should I be worried?

This is a tricky one as you probably don't want Declan's school to label you as a fussy or pushy mum. Remember children develop as readers at different rates and there may be no significance in the fact that Declan is on a lower reading level book than others in his class. He may just be consolidating skills before a phase of quick improvement. Also the junior school can be quite a daunting place. Declan has so much else to cope with (apart from reading and writing) such as remembering to hang up his coat in the right place in the cloakroom and to make sure he gets picked for the football game at playtime!

However, if you are worried then it is best to raise the issue in school as soon as you become aware of it. If you wait, then things might go more wrong for your child and it might be more difficult to put it right.

Ask to see Declan's teacher but, in the first instance, keep the tone light, for example, 'Have you a minute to talk to me about Declan's reading? His dad and I have noticed that he doesn't seem to be making the progress other children are.' Declan's teacher will welcome your interest and your eagerness to help your child. Chances are she will be able to reassure you that all that has happened is that your child has reached a plateau and, for the time being, progress is halted. Don't forget teachers see lots of children and they will see the plateau as a very natural stage for children of your child's age.

Alternatively Declan's teacher may also be puzzled by his current lack of progress. If this is the case, then it is best to devise a strategy for you and the school to work in co-operation. Perhaps the school will suggest you spend more time, in a relaxed way, sharing books with Declan at home. Perhaps they feel you could do more in the way of playing literacy games with him. Be prepared to give the teacher's suggestions every chance of succeeding but agree to meet again after a month to review progress. If after a month you feel you have done your best to be supportive, but you are still concerned, then arrange a time to talk to the teacher more formally. You need to know if the school has concerns about your child's progress and, if so, what they are doing about it? It might be sensible to ask if the special needs co-ordinator (SENCo) or inclusion manager could attend the meeting too. He or she might suggest that Declan joins a small group of children in his year who are under-performing in literacy and they will be given special help (usually by a teaching assistant). Ask the teacher how you can support Declan's reading at home. He or she will probably have lots of suggestions of things you can do to smooth Declan's progress with reading.

Be prepared to put in more time and effort to make reading sessions at home fun and successful for Declan. At home he may need lots of relaxing and stress-free times with books which you share together without expecting him to do the reading. This approach may prove to be more productive than watching him struggle to work out the words on the page. Try to stay calm. If you are anxious, this will communicate itself to Declan and only further hinder his progress.

Summary

If your child is experiencing difficulties with learning to read there are things you can do to help:

- Make sure reading is still a positive and enjoyable experience for him. If hearing him read is too stressful because he makes so many mistakes, then you read to him. This is a very important foundation for all reading skills and you certainly shouldn't do less of it at a time when your child is experiencing difficulties.
- Work in partnership with the school. The school will be doing its best to help your child and they will welcome all offers of support from you. Remember the best support at home might be to offer a complementary range of reading experiences. If the school has in place a systematic revision of core skills of reading such as:
  - accurate phonic blending
  - recognizing words on sight
  - ensuring your child is understanding what he is reading

  then support at home might take the form of:

  - reading to your child
  - talking about books
  - playing word games.

10

children who
can read ... but
don't

In this chapter you will learn:
- why some children give up reading
- whether it matters if children who can read don't bother to read
- what parents can do to encourage their child to read.

Those who read the most, read the best.

US Department of Education, *National Assessment of Educational Progress 2004*

Although politicians get very hot under the collar about falling literacy standards and the British press will always run an alarmist 'decline in literacy' story on a 'slow news' day, the reality is that the vast majority of children are successful readers by the age of seven. Generally, children aged seven can:

- read over 300 words 'on sight'
- blend the sounds of the letters to read unfamiliar words
- talk confidently about what they have read.

However, we do have a real challenge facing us as a society and that is that vast numbers of children who have learned to read, thanks to the dedication of parents and teachers, choose not to read once they are able to do so. It is as if they have perceived 'reading' to be about acquiring the skills of reading and once those have been achieved, they are quite willing to stop reading. Indeed one boy, aged seven, was heard to say exactly that: 'This book is the top level of the scheme and when I've finished it I can stop reading!'

Why some children give up reading

How can it be, that just as we should be launching children to fly solo in the world of reading, they choose to stop reading?

For an answer to this question, parents and teachers need to reflect upon how they have presented reading to children. If the emphasis has been on:

- racing up the levels of the reading scheme
- prioritizing 'getting through' a book as quickly as possible
- concentrating on skills (phonics and quickly recognizing whole words) at the expense of exploring the book's content
- restricting the time spent reading aloud to children and, instead, expecting them to 'do their reading' as a solitary activity

then it is not surprising that children have not cottoned on to what is 'in' reading for them. They have acquired the skills of reading but have not simultaneously developed a love of reading and run the risk of becoming children who can read, but don't.

Of course, it might not just be children who think that once the basic skills of reading have been achieved then there is not much point in persevering with reading! Many parents show less interest in the reading habits of their newly fluent child than they did when that child was at the beginning stages of becoming a reader. The truth of the matter is that if we do not continue to foster in our children an interest in books then the skill will plateau and the sense of enjoyment in books will seriously decline. Like many things in life it's a case of 'use it or lose it'!

What does it matter if a child can read but chooses not to?

> *When children read for pleasure, when they get 'hooked on books', they acquire, involuntarily and without conscious effort, nearly all of the so-called 'language skills' many people are so concerned about ... Although free voluntary reading alone will not ensure attainment of the highest levels of literacy, it will at least ensure an acceptable level. Without it, I suspect that children simply do not have a chance.*

Krashen, *The Power of Reading* (1993)

If children do not persevere with the habit of reading then, from the point of view of their education, a number of things may result. First, their language development will slow down (we are much more likely to adopt new vocabulary when we have read it than if we just hear it in conversation) and, second, their writing development will be seriously affected.

Successful writing depends on what we have read (not what we have said) and if children are not regularly exposed to the patterns of written language then they will have no 'resource bank' of language to call on when they come to write. It's like remembering a tune. The first time you hear a song, you might enjoy it but it's unlikely that you can reproduce it. If you hear it again, you will recognize that you have heard it before but that is not the same as being able to sing it. When you hear it yet again you might be able to sing along with the radio or CD but if, like a karaoke machine, the sound is turned off, you may not be able to continue unaccompanied. Only when you have heard a tune three or four times will the pattern of music and words have impacted on your memory so that you can reproduce them. If children are to have 'an ear' for written language they need to hear it many, many times. They can hear it when they read silently to themselves and they can hear it when you read aloud to them, but without that input children will not know the 'tune of writing'. They will try to 'write as they speak' and that will never result in well-organized and effective writing.

> ... *reading amount and reading achievement are thought to be reciprocally related to each other – as reading amount increases, reading achievement increases, which in turn increases reading amount.*
>
> Cunningham and Stanovich, *What Reading Does for the Mind* (1998)

What can parents do to encourage their children to read?

Read to your child

Although your child can now read independently there is no need to stop reading to them. Most, if not all, adults enjoy being read to although they may not recognize that this is what they are enjoying! When we listen to the news on the radio or enjoy listening to an interview with a film star it is the same as if we were being read to. If parents continue to read to children they are able to entice them into being adventurous in their own book choices. They can read books to their child that would be slightly too difficult for the child to read independently. In this way they are providing an incentive for the child to persevere with their own reading so that, in due course, they will be able to read such books for themselves.

Reading to your child is a particularly effective way to have 'quality time' with her. It apparently makes no demands on her so it is very pleasurable although, in reality, the child is learning about vocabulary and language and also to have a wider understanding about human nature or the world around her, but this learning is very discreet and that is what makes it so powerful.

Use audio books

As well as you reading aloud to your child it is a good idea for her to listen to stories on CDs. When children listen to stories it is a very relaxing way for them to tune in to language. They will enjoy hearing a popular actor giving a dramatized reading of a book. Often children enjoy hearing the same story on CD over and over again. This increases the benefit to their language development as they will already be familiar with the plot and so they will be listening more attentively to the tunes of the language.

Use ebooks

Children are already steeped in hand-held culture. They sometimes seem to use mobile phones, MP3 players and hand-held games consoles as if they were extensions to their own hands! Books, of course, are the ultimate hand-held object but, for some children, the format may not seem as smart as a piece of electronic technology. There are a number of 'ebooks' on the market which are able to offer a reading experience very similar to that of holding a 'real' book but which have the advantage of looking 'cool'. Currently these are quite expensive but inevitably the price will drop and the ebook might be just the thing to tempt a reluctant reader.

Read more than books

It is, of course, important that children have access to the finest that children's literature can offer but nobody would expect them to read that all the time. Adults may enjoy the classics of English literature but also enjoy reading a newspaper or a magazine. Provide a wide range of reading material for your child: comics, computer magazines, football magazines, comic books such as 'Asterix'. Poring over 'solve your own adventure' books in which the reader has to work out clues and crack codes is just as useful as reading material as a longer more challenging novel. Reading such lighter weight material will not make your child lazy or more reluctant to take on the effort of reading more demanding books, but will help her to feel in control of her reading habit instead of being burdened by it.

Make time for reading

It is much easier to encourage your child to continue reading if she is already used to spending time reading. If the window of opportunity for reading closes it will quickly be filled with other leisure activities, most obviously watching TV. Then it will be very difficult to make that time again. Of course, it would be unreasonable to expect children to read if no adults in the home ever spend time reading. Like many things in child-rearing the most effective message is 'do as I do' not just 'do as I say'. In most houses with young children the adults do not have much time to read when the children are up and about. Most of the reading the adults do will go on in the evening after the child have gone to bed. Even avid adult readers can often only read for snatched moments at the end of a busy day. So it may be that your child does not actually witness you doing a lot of book reading. However, if they:

- hear you talk about books
- see books around the home
- go with you to the library
- watch you choose books from the Internet

then they are getting a strong message about how important you think reading is. Choose times to suggest that your child reads which do not mean she is missing out on other things. It is never going to be popular if you turn off her favourite programme and demand that she reads, but the early evening, when most channels are devoted to news and reportage, might be a good time to encourage your child to read.

Read with your child

If your child seems to resent spending time at home reading, then make a deal with her that you will take it in turns to read the pages of a book. Your child will read a page and then you will read the following page. This sharing of the reading takes some of the pressure off your child. It also helps her to hold on to the meaning of the book as the pages you read to her will enable her to follow the plot more easily.

Top tip

Don't be too rigid about the division of the reading. If 'your' page happens to have very few words and 'her' page is a full page of words, you could agree a swap!

Make reading comfortable

Children will need a comfortable place to settle down with their book of the moment. If their concentration has to compete with the television it would be a very avid reader who could shut out the persistence of the sound and images coming from the TV. If possible, make sure there is another room which is comfortable and warm to make reading enticing as a leisure pursuit.

Show an interest in what your child is reading

You don't need to 'hear' your child read any more but that doesn't mean you don't need to take any interest in what she is reading. This 'interest' should not take the form of an 'inquisition' by checking up on how well children are reading, but rather more like the interest of another reader. You might ask:

• What are you reading at the moment?
• Is it any good?
• Have you read anything else by that author?
• What's the best bit?

Encouraging your child to talk about what she is reading will enhance her understanding of the books.

Buy books

Research has shown that children who own books are much more likely to persist with reading after they have first acquired the skill. Children's reading habits differ from those of adults. Many adults enjoy the first read of a book and may not be inclined to ever re-read it. Children, by contrast, often re-read at a phenomenal rate. It would seem that children reap some psychological reward in the comfort of reading what is familiar. Of course, this is much easier for them to do if the books are on their own bookshelves.

Give children a book allowance

If children have to make a choice between spending their pocket money on toys, computer games or books it is probably too difficult a choice to expect them to make, so why not make life easier for them by giving them a separate book allowance? This will help them get into the habit of saving for a special book and making careful choices when they have enough money. All of these behaviours make reading a pastime that is more like children's other hobbies – saving up for something and then browsing in catalogues, websites and bookshops to find new things.

Use your local library

When children become newly fluent as readers they often read books very quickly. This means that a book you have bought them on Saturday morning could be finished by Sunday afternoon! It is best to consider using the local library while your child is going through this stage of reading relatively short books quite quickly. Later on, when your child has more reading stamina, and is reading books of much greater length, a book may last her several weeks but in the meantime the library provides a very convenient way to supply her reading habit. In the children's section of most libraries there will be books that are identified for the seven- to nine-year-old child or the 'newly independent reader'. This is where you and your child should browse to discover what your child likes in a book.

Don't ignore the non-fiction section of the library. Lots of children, particularly boys, enjoy reading non-fiction rather than fiction and the library will have an extensive range of large format books on every topic under the sun (and some on the sun itself!).

Do take advantage of the knowledge of the library staff. Most libraries have a specialist children's librarian whose knowledge of books will be extensive. He or she will be able to find just the right book to tempt your child to read more.

Help your child to choose books

Choosing a book that will be 'just right' is not an easy thing to do, even for an experienced adult reader, but for a child it can be a minefield. If we stop to consider how adults make choices about books and then compare that with the opportunities children may have, it can be quite revealing:

- *Adults often recommend books to one another.* What opportunity does your child have for someone to informally (yet enthusiastically) make suggestions about what they should read next? When a friend says to you, 'You've got to read this book – it's amazing!' that is such an encouragement to seek out the book and enjoy it for yourself. Children may not get much of this friendly advice about books so parents may need to create this for their children. You could ask the advice of a children's librarian or look on the web for suggestions for what other children, the same age as your child, are reading. A book such as *Who Next ...? A Guide to Children's Authors* (see 'Taking it further', page 235) is a very helpful guide for adults to support and extend children's reading.

- *Adults often read (or hear) book reviews.* Many adults are guided to their next book after having heard or read a review of the book. This snippet of information can be just enough to persuade you that you would like to read the book yourself. Most book guides in the newspapers also have a children's section, but chances are your child does not browse these sections of your newspaper and so you will need to cut out some of the reviews and see if the books appeal to your child.
- *Adults know which authors they like.* Many adults read from a relatively narrow range of authors. It is as if we find an author who suits our needs and we may remain very loyal to that author. Children may be much less aware of favourite authors, so if your child has enjoyed a particular book, make a note of the author's name and look out for more books by the same author in the library or bookshop.
- *Adults know which genre they like.* Most adults read from a fairly limited range of genres. Some may read whatever comes their way, but most have a very set idea of the 'kind' of books they like. Bookshops are well aware of this and arrange their books accordingly into categories such as 'romance', 'thriller', 'adventure', 'history', 'horror' or 'sci fi'. Children, who may be used to the school putting the next book they should read into their hands, may have very little idea about which genre appeals to them. Talk to your children about the kinds of books they like – funny stories, school stories, football stories, fantasy stories. Then do a quick search on the web for children's authors and titles of books that come into that category.

Let your child read 'easy' books

There is a danger that parents will expect their children to always be reading at their 'point of learning'. This is a little harsh as most adults do very little reading that is outside their comfort zone. A survey of the reading habits of an avid adult reader is likely to reveal titles that tend to be on the 'easy' side rather than the 'challenging'. So libraries loan (and bookshops sell) far more Barbara Taylor Bradford and Maeve Binchy than Marcel Proust or Charles Dickens! That is not to say that most adults couldn't read the classics but, significantly, they usually choose not to. Children need to have plenty of reading material that is 'easy'. It is by reading lots of books that do not make too many demands on their word recognition skills that children develop reading stamina. That is, the stickability to persevere with a book and not be easily distracted. This skill is acquired through the practice of reading and practice should be pleasurable. If a parent is disparaging about a book – 'You're not reading that babyish thing are you?' – this will devalue the reading that hitherto the child might have been thoroughly enjoying. If your child is enjoying reading something then accept that for what it is. Don't always be looking to 'improve' the quality of your child's reading material. It is likely to put your child off reading altogether and then it can be very hard to woo her back.

Read 'tempters'

The best way to tempt your child to be more adventurous with her book choices is to read aloud to her from books that you know she will enjoy but which might require more dedication from your child if she were to attempt them as solo reads. Once you have read a book to a child two things usually happen:

- Your child wants to read the book for herself.
- Your child has been introduced to an author and she may try another title by the same author.

Don't abandon picture books

You may feel that your seven-year-old has outgrown picture books but you would be wrong. Picture books may seem 'easy' in that they may not have many words on the page but they often deal with subjects that are just as demanding as longer works of fiction. Issues such as falling out with a best friend or getting into trouble can be powerfully conveyed in a book that may only have 24 pages. If you ban the picture book because you think your child should be reading something more weighty, your child may not enjoy reading longer chapter books and, as a result, she may give up on reading altogether.

Go to book events

Bookshops and libraries often arrange a 'book event' which usually means they have invited a particular author to the bookshop to sign books. Children's authors are particularly good at these events and do not restrict themselves to mechanically signing books. They usually give an animated reading of part of their book and are usually willing to answer children's questions (no matter how personal some of those questions might be!). Actually meeting an author can be a great boost to a child's enthusiasm for reading.

Some children prefer non-fiction

Some children, particularly boys, prefer non-fiction to fiction. It is best to recognize these preferences and not try to undermine them. Choose non-fiction books on topics that appeal to your child, for example, cartoon illustrations or keeping a pony.

Some boys respond best to reading when they are given a specific purpose rather than just 'reading' which they may perceive as 'aimless'. If your child is reading a non-fiction book, pose a question such as 'What was the first cartoon Walt Disney illustrated?' or 'What is the maximum size a pony can be to compete in a gymkhana?' These questions will direct your child back into the book to search for the answers. It will keep his interest in the book alive and will also show him that you share that interest.

Of course, one of the appeals of non-fiction to boys might be that non-fiction is clearly structured and many boys like systems and structure (hence the appeal of Lego building!). If we guide them towards fiction that has a clear structure, for example, solving a mystery or choose-your-own adventure, we may find boys just as interested in fiction.

Feed their curiosity for the foul and revolting!

Many children have an endless fascination for topics that most adults find repellent – dirt and all things disgusting are often high on the popularity list for children aged between 8 and 11. There are lots of books (many of them conveniently arranged in extensive sets such as 'Horrible Histories') that pander to children's interest in the gory and gruesome and there is no point being superior about this aspect of children's reading tastes.

If it appeals to them, they will read it, and it is better that they are reading something than allowing their reading skills to atrophy and fade.

Follow the hobby

Some parents say that their children have 'no time for reading' because their lives are so filled with other hobbies, but that's the amazing thing about reading – it fits with any hobby. There are stories, information books and magazines about any possible hobby a child could enjoy. For the very 'book-averse' boy even reading the facts on Top Trump cards is at least reading and is better than not reading anything!

Follow the TV/Film

In bookshops there is usually a whole section devoted to books that link with films and TV. These are either:

- the book of the film/TV programme (with the film being released first – sometimes called the 'novelization')
- the film/TV programme of the book (with the book being released first)
- the book of the making of the film.

Adults enjoy reading something they have seen first on screen and children are no different. Children who generally choose non-fiction books can sometimes be tempted to read a fiction text when they already know the plot (Harry Potter books are a particularly good example of this and there are many boys whose only fiction reading is Harry Potter although they may devour many non-fiction books). If the book is published after the film (or to coincide with the release of the film) the publishers often produce a range of books to link with the film. Some of these have more visuals than others (often with 'stills' from the film) and this can be very appealing to the 'book-shy' child. For example, there are lots of books to accompany the film series 'Indiana Jones' – a book about the making of the film; an 'ultimate guide'; an annual; a 'photographic journey' as well as numerous 'novelizations'.

Suggest your child's school holds a book fair

A number of publishing organizations offer 'book fairs' to be held in schools, for example, Scholastic, Usborne, Jubilee Books and

Travelling Books, to name but a few. Generally the publishers supply a collection of books for the school to sell (on sale or return). The books are available for sale in the school for a week. The school has to organize the actual selling (taking the money, etc.) and this usually takes place at lunch time or after school.

The idea of buying a book while your friends are also buying books is very appealing to children and they are often swept along with a general enthusiasm which can overcome the reluctance of even the most hesitant book chooser.

In some schools the organization of the book fair is the responsibility of the parent/teacher association (PTA). Find out if your PTA is planning such an event. If they are, make sure you attend. If not, then encourage them to have one.

The publishers offer discounts to the school on every book sold. This means that, while the parent pays the list price, the school is getting money on every sale which goes towards replenishing the school library for the benefit of all the children in the school.

Holiday reading

Many adults find the bulk of their relaxation reading is restricted to holidays and the busy bookshops at every airport bear witness to this. Indeed, there are 'airport editions' of many popular titles that are sold exclusively in airport departure lounges!

Holidays are a good time for parents to spend more time reading to their children. The hectic schedule of homework, after-school clubs and preparing for work the next day is relaxed for a week or so and both adults and children can make more time for reading.

This is a very good opportunity to select a longer book that you will read a few chapters of each evening. This sense of a plot unfolding in 'episodes' is a very engaging experience for all readers. Back in Victorian times, Charles Dickens made good use of this technique, making his readers all the more eager as they had to wait for the next instalment. Indeed, in the winter of 1841, American fans in New York, desperate to learn the fate of Little Nell (from *The Old Curiosity Shop*) thronged the docks and shouted out to the incoming passengers from across the Atlantic: 'Is Little Nell dead?' (She was!)

For your holiday read-aloud:

- choose a book that will last the holiday (as best as you can judge it)
- encourage all your children to listen, from the oldest to the youngest
- read aloud every evening (if at all possible)
- make your reading as polished as possible (for tips on reading aloud see Chapter 01)
- ensure everyone is sitting comfortably
- have no other distractions (music, TV, computer)
- choose a book that is just above the independent reading level of your oldest child. This might be a long way above the comprehension level of your youngest child but, with any luck, they will be mesmerized by the communal feeling of enjoyment that everyone else is experiencing. (Also you could bribe them by reading several of 'their' books first, before the 'proper' reading aloud session begins!)
- talk about the book during the day. Speculate (and encourage your children to speculate) about how things might turn out in the book.

One family with three children aged between seven and 11 had a tradition of reading aloud from a longer novel every evening of their camping holidays. One holiday the weather was atrocious and, after a particularly bad night, they decided to pack up and go home. As they dismantled the tent they were approached by an older couple. The couple were dismayed to see the family preparing to leave. 'But you can't go,' they said. 'We have to hear the end of the story!' It turned out that, each evening, as the mum read aloud she had also been entertaining the couple whose caravan was parked next to their tent! The spirit of Dickens and the desire to know what happens next is alive and well!

Enlist the help of grandparents

Encourage grandparents to read to their grandchildren. This is a particularly pleasant way to further the bonds of friendship between the generations and, at some points in life, grandparents may have more time to spend reading and talking about books with their grandchildren.

Read and do

Some children prefer books that lead directly into some activity, such as model making or cooking. Do not underestimate the value of this kind of reading. It is very practical and it also makes considerable demands upon comprehension. Being able to read a recipe and then make the cake is not only a life skill but it is also very satisfying (particularly if the cake turns out well!).

And finally … if all else fails …

Try bribery!

It may be a last resort but you might consider bribing your child to read more. It need not be quite as despicable as it sounds if you make it part of a challenge with a reward (or prize). Agree with your child that she will read a certain number of books in a certain space of time. (Don't be overly ambitious but set a pace that will require some commitment from your child.)

Set out the terms of the challenge very clearly, for example, to read five books in a month. Make everything as easy as you can for your child. Help her to choose the books and, ideally, have all five available at the start of the challenge. Write the title on a chart with some spaces for dates. Encourage your child to write on the chart the page reference and the date. When a book is finished tick the box and show progress up a scale (towards the final reward). This could be a thermometer rising or a star (building up to a five-star award). When your child has read a book you should sit and chat to her about it but don't turn it into an interrogation! Ask a few 'open' questions such as, 'What was the most exciting bit?' 'Was there any part which took you by surprise?' Allow your child to handle the book and find her way around it for the answers (it's not supposed to be a memory test!). Encourage your child to give the book a score out of ten. Then start the next book.

Be prepared to help your child. If she asks you to read some of the book to her, do so willingly. After all, your goal is for your child to engage more with books not to slog through the texts just for the prize at the end.

When all five books have been read have a celebration – perhaps you could make her a special tea or encourage a call to grandparents to fill them in on the reading progress. You could offer a cash reward for her to buy whatever she likes, or you could offer 'double the money' if she chooses to spend the prize on books! Don't put any pressure on her to choose the book option. She has worked hard for her prize and she deserves to spend it however she pleases. Let a month or so go by before you propose another book challenge.

This may seem a very mercenary way to tempt children into something that we might think they should do without any incentive, but children have a lot of calls on their time and part of 'getting the reading habit' is having time in your life when reading happens. If you have to engineer to have this time, then so be it. The hope is that as your child reads more, books work their magic and what started as a chore becomes a pleasure and before you know it you don't need the chart (although the need for money for books will probably continue!).

Summary

- The more children read, the better readers and writers they will be.
- Children may easily give up the reading habit if parents don't support it.
- There are lots of ways to tempt children back into reading.

appendix 1

The 44 phonemes in the English language

There are 24 consonant phonemes and 20 vowel phonemes.

The 24 consonant phonemes

Eighteen consonant letter phonemes

b (bat)	c/k (cat, kick)	d (dog)	f (fish)	g (goat)	h (he)
j (jam)	l (lid)	m (mud)	n (nut)	p (pot)	r (rat)
s (see)	t (top)	v (vat)	w (water)	y (yet)	z (zebra)

Six further consonant phonemes (digraphs)

ch (chop) ng (sing) th (then) th (thin) sh (ship) zh (television, measure)

The 20 vowel phonemes

Five short vowel phonemes

a (cat) e (pet) i (big) o (dog) u (nut)

Five long vowel phonemes:

ay (cake) ee (me) igh (night) oa (boat) oo (rule)

Ten further vowel phonemes

ar (car)	er (term)	or (port)	oo (book)	ow (how)
oi (boy)	air (hair)	ear (hear)	ure (pure)	uh (letter)

Advice when pronouncing the 44 sounds

Some letters are easy to 'sound out' because even when they are 'extended', for example, 'sssss', the sound is not distorted.

Some letters are difficult to 'sound out' because it is hard to pronounce them without adding an 'extra' sound. The 'explosive' letters like 'b' 'c' 'd' 'g' 'p' and 't' are difficult to say without adding 'uh' on the end – 'b-uh'; 'c-uh', etc.

When sounding out words for children we should make the sounds as they occur in the word. So, for example, the word 'bird' has three sounds: b/ur/d (not b/i/r/d); and the word 'shoe' has two sounds: sh/oe.

The 100 most frequently used words

The following 12 words account for approximately 25 per cent of all the words we read:

a	and	he	I	in	is
it	of	that	the	to	was

The following 20 words account for about a further 10 per cent of all the words we read:

all	are	as	at	be	but
for	had	have	him	his	not
on	one	said	so	they	we
with	you				

The following 68 words account for another 20 per cent of all the words we read:

about	an	back	been	before	big
by	call	came	can	come	could
did	do	down	first	from	get
go	has	her	here	if	into
just	like	little	look	made	make
me	more	much	must	my	new
no	now	off	old	only	or
other	our	out	over	saw	see
she	some	their	them	then	there
this	to	up	want	well	went
were	what	when	where	which	who
will	your				

appendix 3

Mirror writing passage

Here is what the passage on page 141 reads:

Learning to read is not easy. Although a great deal of research has been undertaken into how children learn to read this by no means guarantees that all children will become readers effortlessly. What research does reveal is that it is essential for children to understand that the reason for learning to read is for them to get meaning from texts. If parents demonstrate the pleasure they get from reading and if they support their child's reading in a happy and relaxed situation, they can have an enormous impact on their child's journey to reading.

appendix 4

Sentences to contextualize high frequency words

He saw a big dog.
That is not my book.
I have a new game.
We all went to the football match.
They can see an old car.

NB All nouns should be shown with a small picture.

taking it further

Perhaps after reading this book, some parents or carers would like to know more about aspects of helping their child with reading. The list of books, websites, resources and organizations in this chapter should help you find what you need or at least point you in the right direction.

Useful organizations

The National Literacy Trust (NLT)
www.literacytrust.org.uk
This is an independent charity dedicated to promoting literacy and includes the following projects:

- **Reading is Fundamental (RIF)**
  www.rif.org.uk
  This initiative promotes a love of reading among children and young people (aged 0–19) in areas of disadvantage and gives them the chance to choose free books to keep.
- **Talk To Your Baby**
  www.talktoyourbaby.org.uk
  This is a campaign run by the NLT to encourage parents and carers to talk more to children from birth to three years of age.
- **Bookstart**
  www.bookstart.org.uk
  This is the world's first national baby book gifting programme. Through National Health Service (NHS) health visitors it provides every baby in the UK with a free Bookstart pack of books and guidance materials that encourage the use of the local library. The leaflet included, 'Babies Love Books', gives advice on sharing books with your baby.

- **Storysack**

  www.storysack.com

  This project encourages parents and carers to share stories with their children. Adults are advised on how to choose a book and then to fill a cloth bag (hence the name!) with toys, props and scenery that can be used to bring the book to life. For example, the Storysack of 'Goldilocks and the Three Bears' might include a puppet bear, a toy bed, three plastic bowls for porridge and a toy chair.

The British Dyslexia Association (BDA)

www.bdadyslexia.org.uk

The BDA defines dyslexia as

> a specific learning difficulty which mainly affects the development of literacy and language related skills. It is likely to be present at birth and to be lifelong in its effects. It is characterized by difficulties with phonological processing, rapid naming, working memory, processing speed, and the automatic development of skills that may not match up to an individual's other cognitive abilities. It tends to be resistant to conventional teaching methods, but its effects can be mitigated by appropriately specific intervention, including the application of information technology and supportive counselling.

The BDA offers information and advice on supporting those with dyslexia. The website also has a link to an online dyslexia screening test (for which there is a £30 fee).

The International Dyslexia Association

www.interdys.org

This non-profit organization has branches throughout the USA.

I CAN

www.ican.org.uk

I CAN is a charity that aims to improve children's speech, language and communication skills. Talking Point (www.ican.org.uk/talkingpoint) has useful information for parents on developing these skills in their child.

Useful websites

www.parentlineplus.org.uk (0808 800 2222) is a national UK charity that works for and with parents.

www.bbc.co.uk/cbeebies has a tab for 'Grown-ups' that includes useful background reading such as 'Listening, Speaking and Literacy' by Sue Palmer.

www.teachit.co.uk/attachments/7359.pdf This helpful website explains why some sounds of the English language are particularly difficult for children to hear and reproduce.

Useful books

The development of children's language

How Children Learn Language by William O'Grady (Cambridge University Press, 2005, ISBN: 978-0521531924)
This book is primarily intended for students of child language development but its easy anecdotal style makes it an interesting read for parents too.

Listen to Your Child: A Parent's Guide to Children's Language by David Crystal (Penguin, 1999, ISBN: 978-0140110159)
This fascinating book gives parents an insight into the development of children's language from birth to early school years.

The Meaning Makers: Children Learning Language and Using Language to Learn by Gordon Wells (Heinemann, 1985, ISBN: 978-0435082475)
This academic book is based on a study the author undertook in Bristol tracking children's language development from their first words to the end of primary education.

Talk and Listen Together (Basic Skills Agency, 2003, ISBN: 978-1859902417)
This £5 pack is for parents and young children aged 0–3. It offers lots of practical ideas for activities to do together.

Baby signing

Baby Signs: How to Talk with Your Baby Before Your Baby Can Talk by Linda Acredolo and Susan Goodwyn (McGraw-Hill, 2009, ISBN: 978-0071615037)
This is the third edition of this popular book drawing on the research of the authors who were at the University of California. It is based on American Sign Language (ASL).

Complete Guide to Baby Signing by Joseph Garcia (Match Media Publishing, 2004, ISBN: 978-1904840008)
This comprehensive guide to baby signing is quite expensive and many parents have found they can get the hang of baby signing with shorter (and cheaper) books of which there are many on the market.

My First Signs by Annie Kubler (Child's Play, 2004, ISBN: 978-1904550044)
This 12-page board book describes the first basic signs based on British Sign Language (BSL). It obviously goes into far less detail than the more academic books but if you plan to take your baby to baby signing classes in the UK, these are likely to teach BSL.

Theory of learning

Jean Piaget was a Swiss philosopher who in the 1950s mapped four levels of cognitive development in children: sensorimotor stage (0–2); preoperational stage (2–7); concrete operational stage (7–11); and formal operational stage (11+).

The book *How Children Learn* by Linda Pound (Step Forward Publishing, 2005, ISBN: 978-1904575092) reviews a variety of different theories of child development, including Piaget. The book is intended for early years practitioners but parents may find the background information interesting.

Thought and Language: The Zone of Proximal Development by L. S. Vygotsky (MIT Press, 1962)
Although the focus of this academic book is not children learning to talk and read, in Vygotsky's theory of the zone of proximal development he describes how learners best acquire new skills in the company of others who are already skilled, which provides an excellent model for the parent-child role when sharing books.

Literacy from Home to School: 'Reading with Alice' by Robin Campbell (Trentham Books Ltd, 1998, ISBN: 978-1858561660)
This is an observation of one child and her relationship with print, from birth until she goes to school. The author, who is the child's grandfather, documents the stages of her development and explains what it can teach teachers and parents.

Learning to read

Help Your Child to Read and Write by Fiona Chandler (Usborne, 2008, ISBN: 978-0746084434)
This book in the Usborne 'Parents' Guides' series is full of practical advice.

Helping Your Child to Read: A Parent's Handbook for the Oxford Reading Tree Series by Kate Ruttle and Annemarie Young (Oxford University Press, 2005, ISBN: 978-0198385660)
This book accompanies the Oxford Reading Tree reading scheme. It is for parents to support their children's reading at home.

How to Help Your Child Read and Write by Dominic Wyse (Prentice Hall Life, 2007, ISBN: 978-1405840248)

How to Help Your Child Succeed at School by Dominic Wyse (Prentice Hall Life, 2007, ISBN: 978-0273714033)

These two books cover all the major issues about how to help children learn to read and make good progress at school.

Phonics

Introducing rhymes

This Little Puffin, compiled by Elizabeth Matterson (Puffin, 2002, ISBN: 978-0140340488)
This very useful and comprehensive collection of songs, rhymes and games will be invaluable to parents who need to brush up on the words of 'The Wheels on the Bus'!

Action rhymes

There are lots of books containing action rhymes. The easiest way to track them down is to do an Internet search for 'Action Rhymes' and take your pick!

Letters and sounds

The UK Primary National Strategy has produced a publication for schools called 'Letters and Sounds', which describes the stages of development of phonological knowledge. The pack includes a DVD that demonstrates how to pronounce each separate phoneme (letter sound). If you are in the UK, enquire at your local school to see if they could lend you the DVD so that you can practise enunciating the separate sounds accurately.

Jolly Phonics is a synthetic phonics scheme used in many schools. It has a useful guide for parents describing how the scheme works. See the website for further information:

www.jollylearning.co.uk/2007_UKGuide.pdf

Read Write Inc.

This synthetic phonics scheme has a free downloadable parent's booklet to accompany the Read Write Inc. programme. See www.readwriteinc.com/page12.html

Reading aloud to your child

'The Reading Mother', a poem by the American poet Strickland Gillilan in the anthology *The Best Loved Poems of the American People*, edited by Hazel Felleman (Doubleday & Co Inc., 1936, ISBN: 978-0385000192)

How to Enjoy Reading Aloud to Young Children by Edmund Pegge and Alison Shakspeare (Southgate Publishers, 2007, ISBN: 978-1857411560)
This booklet is full of practical tips on how to read aloud to children.

The Read-Aloud Handbook by Jim Trelease (Penguin, 2006, ISBN: 978-0143037392)
This handbook on reading aloud to children of all ages is now in its sixth edition and no wonder! It is an invaluable and practical guide for all parents on how to sow the seeds for a child to become an avid reader. The style is clear and informal with plenty of insightful anecdotes. It also includes a treasury of books suitable for reading aloud.

Reading Magic: Why Reading Aloud to Our Children Will Change Their Lives Forever by Mem Fox (Harvest Books, 2001, ISBN: 978-0156011556)
This very readable little book will convince any parent of the value of spending time reading aloud to their children.

Advice on choosing books for your child

Join the library! Membership of all libraries is free and open to all. To join, you simply go along to any library and bring some ID with you. All libraries have special sections with children's books and specially trained staff who will be only too pleased to help you make good selections of books for your child.

Libraries also hold 'Story Telling' sessions for young children as well as quizzes and competitions for older children. So make the most of your local library.

Specialist children's bookshops

There are a number of bookshops in the UK that specialize in children's books, for example, **Madeleine Lindley** (www.madeleinelindley.com).

Generally these bookshops will be able to give very useful advice on book choices for children of all ages.

Book guides

Babies Need Books: Sharing the Joy of Books with Children from Birth to Six by Dorothy Butler (Butterworth-Heinemann Ltd, 1982, ISBN: 978-0435081447)

This book was first published in 1980 but it has regularly been revised and it has a wealth of useful advice for parents sharing books with their child.

Guide to Kids' Books (Waterstone's, 2008, ISBN: 978-1902603551)

The Ultimate First Book Guide: Over 500 Great Books for 0–7s by Leonie Flynn, Daniel Hahn and Susan Reuben (A & C Black, 2008, ISBN: 978-0713673319)

The Ultimate Book Guide: Over 600 Great Books for 8–12s by Leonie Flynn, Daniel Hahn and Susan Reuben (A & C Black, 2009, ISBN: 978-1408104385)

Who Next ...? A Guide to Children's Authors by Mary Yardley and Vivian Warren (LISU, 2007, ISBN: 978-1905499069)

Bilingual books

There are many organizations that specialize in bilingual books and if you key in 'bilingual books for children' to any Internet search engine it will come up with a selection of sites, for example:

www.little-linguist.co.uk
www.mothertonguebooks.co.uk

Alternatively you could explore a publisher that specializes in bilingual books, for example, **www.mantra.lingua.com**

'Sharing Stories Together' (Centre for Literacy in Primary Education, 2003, ISBN: 978-8772262270) is a booklet available in English and nine other community languages.

Book clubs

There are a number of book clubs that specialize in selecting books for children aged 0–12. This can be an economical way to extend your child's library as these companies often have very attractive joining offers. Some examples are:

Books for Children
www.bfcbooksdirect.co.uk

The Book People
www.thebookpeople.co.uk

Red House Books
www.redhouse.co.uk

In 2008 Puffin, the children's book division of Penguin Books, relaunched **Puffin Post**, its magazine and book club for children aged 7–12. The Club was first launched in 1967 by Kaye Webb and membership was 10 shillings a year! The Club fizzled out in the early 1980s but it is now back and hoping to attract a new generation of young readers. The annual membership fee is now £45 but for that you get six magazines per year plus six books. Fore more information go to www.puffinpost.co.uk

TV and young children

Dr D. Christakis of the University of Washington in Seattle undertook a study into the effects on babies of lengthy periods of TV 'watching'. His study suggested that early television exposure is associated with attention problems at age seven. He recommended that efforts to limit television viewing in early childhood may be warranted, but called for additional research in this field. See 'Early television exposure and subsequent attentional problems in children' (*Pediatrics*, April 2004, 113[4], pp. 708–13). See also 'Viewing television before age 3 is not the same as viewing television at age 5, D. A. Christakis and F. J. Zimmerman (*Pediatrics*, 1 July 2006, 118[1], pp. 435–6)

In an article in *Time* magazine in 2007, Alice Park reported a study into 'baby videos', which Christakis found were as likely to inhibit the development of language as to extend it. The article also quotes Dr Vic Strasburger on the harmful effects of TV on babies. See www.time.com/time/health/article/0,8599,1650352,00.html

Detoxing Childhood: What Parents Need to Know to Raise Happy, Successful Children by Sue Palmer (Orion, 2007, ISBN: 978-0752890104)

While the scope of this book is much wider than guiding children along the path to become happy and successful readers, it does have some very useful sections on the harm that can be done when children's television viewing is taken to excess.

'Television and DVD/Video Viewing in Children: Younger Than 2 Years' (2007), a study by Frederick J. Zimmerman, PhD; Dimitri A. Christakis, MD, MPH; and Andrew N. Meltzoff, PhD. See http://ilabs.washington.edu/news/UW_I-Labs_infant_TV_ viewing.pdr.pdf

How to Stop Your Kids Watching Too Much TV by Teresa Orange and Louise O'Flynn (Hay House Inc., 2007, ISBN: 978-1401915476)

This book offers practical methods for reducing screen-time and ideas for other more productive activities.

Remotely Controlled: How Television is Damaging Our Lives by Aric Sigman (Vermilion, 2007, ISBN: 978-1904550044)

This outspoken account of the damage TV viewing may be having on you and your child makes for worrying reading!

The following web page has more information:
www.raisesmartkid.com/articles/the-effects-of-tv-on-baby.html

References

'Early father's and mother's involvement and child's later educational outcomes' by E. Flouri and A. Buchanan (*British Journal of Educational Psychology*, 2004, vol. 74, pp. 141–53)

Listen to Your Child: A Parent's Guide to Children's Language by David Crystal (Penguin, 1989, ISBN: 978-0140110159)

Mr. Gumpy's Outing by John Burningham (Red Fox, 2001, ISBN: 978-0099408796)

Proust and the Squid: The Story and Science of the Reading Brain by Maryanne Wolf (Icon Books, 2008, ISBN: 978-1848310308)

'Reading aloud to children: the evidence' by Barry Zuckerman (*Archives of Disease in Childhood*, May 2008)

Under Pressure: Rescuing our Children from the Culture of Hyper-parenting by Carl Honoré (Orion, 2008, ISBN: 978-0752891361)

index